RUSSELL BRAND

TANITH CAREY

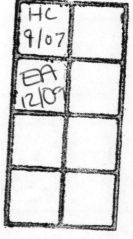

Michael O'Mara Books Limited

First published in 2007 by
Michael O'Mara Books Limited
9 Lion Yard
Tremadoc Road
London SW4 7NQ

A CIP catalogue record for this book is available from the British Library.

ISBN: 978-1-84317-240-6

1 3 5 7 9 10 8 6 4 2

Designed and typeset by E-Type
Plate section designed by Button Group plc

Printed and bound in Great Britain by Clays Ltd, St Ives plc

www.mombooks.com

CONTENTS

AUTHOR'S ACKNOWLEDGEMENTS

Many thanks to the large number of people who helped me write this book. In no particular order – and for many varied reasons – they include Russell's first girlfriend Melanie Gillingham, his inspiring teacher Denis Noonan of the Italia Conti Academy, and the Academy itself, and Christopher Fettes, founder of Drama Centre, who spotted Russell's early potential as a character actor.

From his time at Grays School, Claire Honeywell, Cheryl Benton, Alan Goodwin, Colin Hill, Theresa Cross, Ricky Doye and many others all had fascinating insights. Russell's former manager Nigel Klarfeld was also very helpful, as were Geoff Atkinson and Will Knott from Vera Productions. The same goes for Wendy Danvers, Paul Darby and comedy supremo Karen Koren. I'm grateful to Søren Bonnelle and Uffe Korsemann for giving me a first glimpse of Russell selling chewing gum, and to Vershana and Radha Mohan of the Hare Krishna movement.

Others who came to my aid were Sam at Essex County Council, and the press office of the Hackney Empire.

Plus, for inspiration and support, my thanks go to Graham Brough, Grace Saunders, Paul Field, Ian Vogler, Andrew Wilson, Rich Gowthorpe, Douglas Carnall, Peter Willis and Clare Raymond. I would also like to acknowledge the fans on the Russell Brand Forum, who have shown such intelligent devotion to their idol.

Many other people gave their time, helped me with my research and shared their memories, but would prefer to stay anonymous.

Then, of course, there is Heather Holden-Brown and James Pryor at HHB, who made it all happen. At Michael O'Mara Books, I would like to thank Lindsay Davies, and Kate Gribble for being so efficient and helpful, and Michael himself.

Huge thanks must also go to my husband, Anthony Harwood, who makes all things possible, and to Lily and Clio, who have been so patient.

Finally, there is Russell himself. Thanks for being such an intelligent and captivating subject. I hope I have done you justice.

Tanith Carey
London, 2007

PICTURE ACKNOWLEDGEMENTS

Page 1: Reproduced by kind permission of Melanie Gillingham

Page 2: Reproduced by kind permission of the Italia Conti Academy

Page 3: Detail of a page reproduced from the *Thurrock Gazette* (above); © BBC (below)

Page 4: FremantleMedia (above); Tanith Carey (below)

Page 5: Stills from STIMOROL Chewing Gum advert reproduced by kind permission of Cadbury Schweppes PLC

Page 6: EMPICS (above); www.mirrorpix.com (below)

Page 7: Ian Allis / Capital Pictures

Page 8: Reproduced by kind permission of Wendy Danvers

Page 9: Yemi Shodipo / Famous

Page 10: Steven Parsons / PA / Empics

Page 11: www.mirrorpix.com (above); David Mepham / WENN (below left); Stuart Atkins / Rex Features (below right)

Page 12: Jani Jance / Darren Starling / www.bigpicturesphoto.com

Page 13: Jason Levin / Mark Milan / www.bigpicturesphoto.com (above); Richard Young / Rex Features (below)

Page 14: James Fox / www.expresspictures.com (above); Garaint Lewis / Rex Features (below)

Page 15: Justin Palmer / www.bigpicturesphoto.com (above); David Fisher / Rex Features (below)

Page 16: www.wireimage.com (above); Dave Hogan / Getty Images (below)

FOREWORD

Every so often, there comes a moment when a star is created in front of your eyes. Viewers who tuned into BBC1 witnessed such a scene on *Friday Night with Jonathan Ross* on 12 May 2006. Along with Uma Thurman and Sir Ian McKellen, a cult comedian called Russell Brand was booked to appear. What followed was one of the most frank, provocative and confessional interviews ever seen on British television.

By turns, Russell stunned, amused and appalled with tales of drugs and sexual excess, all delivered in the mangled grammar of a Victorian cad. It was unlike anything the British public had ever heard. With an image that was part Casanova, part Kenneth Williams, Russell was also unlike anything they had ever seen.

Yet somehow it all worked. Those viewers who weren't confused, were intrigued. After fifteen spellbinding minutes, Russell sealed his arrival as the most original comic talent of his generation, when Ross announced the interview had been his best ever with a British comedian.

Such was the impact of the performance, it might have seemed as if Russell had joined the celebrity A-list overnight. In fact, that moment was the culmination of years of hard work by a man determined to make it to the top, an aspiration born the second he had stepped foot on stage in a school production at the age of fifteen.

To that end, Russell first trained as a classical actor and

was hailed as one of the most promising and original talents of his peer group. When he found that he was more interested in saying his own words than following a script, he launched a career as a stand-up comedian. Back then, Russell was not always the funniest on the bill – but he was usually the most memorable. Within a year, he had been discovered at the Edinburgh Fringe Festival and was set on his way to TV stardom as a presenter on MTV.

But, for a time, Russell confused fame with notoriety. As he mimicked his tragic heroes like Richard Pryor and Peter Cook, he sank so low into drug-taking and depravity that, by the age of twenty-seven, it looked like his career was over before it had even got going. From those depths – and partly thanks to the sheer force of his ambition – he managed to beat addictions to heroin, crack and alcohol. With almost as much difficulty, he managed to rebuild his reputation.

Russell's master stroke came when he found the confidence to match his looks with his personality. In the summer of 2005, he set about creating an image that would set him apart from the rest. Once seen, the revamped Russell was never forgotten.

As it turned out, 2006 was finally Russell's year. After almost a decade orbiting celebrity, his stars aligned at last, thanks not only to hard work, but also a short-lived but timely liaison with supermodel Kate Moss. No one else in the history of modern British celebrity has ever achieved such penetration of TV, radio and newspapers so rapidly. In the space of just eight months, Russell fronted four different television programmes (*Big Brother's Big Mouth, One Leicester Square, Russell Brand's Got Issues* and *The Russell Brand Show*), as well as two weekly radio shows, for 6 Music and Radio 2. The same year, he brought out a live comedy DVD, filmed a role in a Hollywood movie, wrote a radio sitcom pilot, and embarked on a punishing national stand-up tour.

Britain became a nation polarized by its opinions on Russell. Newspaper columnists debated his charms. Soon, everyone thought they knew his story – his drug use, his sacking from MTV for dressing as Osama bin Laden, his sex addiction ...

But as one of the most fascinating characters to emerge in Britain for years, Russell is a mass of contradictions. Confessional he may be, but he still struggles to find the answers to some of his own dilemmas. He is adored by women, but says he is lonely. He managed to give up booze and heroin, but struggled to wean himself off sex. He performs as if he is on crack, but a single sip of coffee keeps him awake all night. He says he loves life, but is obsessed by death.

As you will see, Russell's journey from cult comedian to national treasure is far more complex and revealing than even Russell has been prepared to disclose.

CHAPTER ONE

TROUBLED BEGINNINGS

'I wanted a textbook Dickensian

chocolate-box childhood.'

— RUSSELL BRAND ON *RE:BRAND*,

SPRING 2002

With his hair piled high into an impressive quiff, the clean-cut boy grinned broadly from the pages of the local newspaper. Russell Brand was eighteen. He had just landed his first proper TV part – and he wanted the world to know it.

It may have been just a supporting role in a kids' show. But in Russell's mind, it was the first step towards reaching his goal, which lay far beyond the small screen. This Essex boy, as he told the *Thurrock Gazette*, was going to be 'a movie star'.

To his old school friends back in Grays, Essex, it seemed like a bit of an optimistic boast – even for someone with Russell's gigantic self-confidence.

It would be fair to say that Grays, a medium-sized town on a junction of the M25, was not the most obvious springboard for global stardom. With a horizon dominated by the belching chimneys at Tilbury docks, it was a little piece of the East End that had floated down the river – a mass of sprawling Lego-house estates, linked by ring roads and roundabouts. Even when Essex became a byword for Thatcherite consumerism, Grays still seemed to miss out – until the eventual arrival of Lakeside Shopping Centre, when Russell was fifteen. As Russell later put it, Grays was 'ordinary mundane suburbia'. And for as long as he could remember, he had wanted to escape.

There wasn't anything in Russell's immediate background to suggest that acting or comedy would be his way out. There were certainly no actors or comedians in his close family. The nearest his relatives had come to having anything to do with the entertainment world was Russell's great-grandfather on his mum's side, Frederick William Nichols, who made a living making pianos in Hackney. In the forties, the family had done what tens of thousands of other East Enders had done when they found the money. They moved out to the Essex suburbs.

Russell's grandfather, also called Frederick, worked as a salesman and part-time fireman in Hackney during World War Two. Fred met and married his second wife Nellie when she was working as a clothier's clerk. They married in 1942. By the time they had Russell's mum, Barbara, four years later, they had gone up in the world and moved to a comfortable family home in Seymour Gardens, Ilford.

It was a similar story on Russell's dad Ron's side. Russell's late grandfather, Harry, had been a lorry driver in nearby Dagenham, home of the Ford Motor plant. Harry's wife, Russell's grandmother Jen, was also an East Ender through and through. She was born in Commercial Road and grew up in Limehouse, where her dad William was a railway porter. Russell's dark hair and eyes may be partially explained by the fact that Jen's mother, Maud, was of Italian extraction. Her maiden name was Corrotti – and it was believed she was descended from an Italian sculptor of the same name.

Harry was the sort of man who liked to get things done. When he was told he could have a risky operation to sort out his stomach ulcers, he immediately agreed. It was to prove a fatal mistake. He haemorrhaged badly during the surgery and died. It was 1950, and it left Jen a widow with three children – Ron and his two older sisters, Joanne and Janet – to bring up. A dressmaker by trade, Jen did her best to get by, making their clothes and forcing the small amount she earned to stretch as far as it could. She later worked as a receptionist at a local company, before finally marrying again, aged sixty, to a packing-case-maker called Albert Bright.

Despite her trials, Jen was a friendly, vivacious woman who was the life and soul of the street. It was Jen – and her home – which were always to be the calm refuge in Russell's life when times got tough.

The fact that Russell sought sanctuary in years to come was in part down to the ill-starred marriage of his mother Barbara and father Ron. On their wedding day at St Michael's and All Angels church in Gidea Park, Romford, on 5 December 1969, the couple had looked well suited. In their wedding picture, Ron is to the fore, dressed in a sharp brown suit with a red carnation in his buttonhole, his brown hair slicked back. With the same oblong face, defined cheekbones and penetrating brown eyes, the resemblance to Russell is unmistakable. Standing slightly behind her new husband with her head inclined towards him, Babs gives a broad gap-tooth smile. Her twinkling eyes are set off by a glossy brown Mary Quant bob and a voluminous white net veil and tiara.

At twenty-six, Ron Brand was a charmer, who eventually passed on to his son not only his way with words, but also his way with women. He would later remark that Russell's success with the female sex could be put down to 'genes'. He was an Essex boy before the term was invented. Tall, with a charismatic personality and chatty 'All right, mate' manner, Ron always had a plan on how he was going to make his first million. A talented sportsman in his youth, he played local league soccer – and had once been eyed up by West Ham football scouts. Over the years, he was to try his hand at everything from selling water filters, to market trading and communications companies. Yet as soon as he got successful at one thing, Ron got bored and moved on. After Barbara, he was to marry twice more – each time to a woman more than fourteen years his junior.

At twenty-three, his bride Barbara Elizabeth Nichols – or Babs, as she preferred to be known – was just three years younger and had already started working as a secretary. She had a dry wit complemented by an infectious and conspiratorial giggle and was immaculately groomed: every one of Babs's outfits was always coordinated down to the last detail. There was never a chip on her nail varnish or a hair out of place.

At the time of their wedding, Ron was still living with his mum. But the newly-weds soon found a pleasant three-bedroom house with a generous-sized garden a couple of miles away in Grays, just a short drive from the M25 turn-off. Grays End Close was a quiet cul-de-sac of semis, finished in the late fifties. It was the kind of place where they held a street party for the Queen's Jubilee – and you looked out for your neighbours' kids.

By now, Ron was already working on the first of many business ventures. He was running his own photographic studio and processing lab, B and R Photos, named after his own and Barbara's initials, a few miles down the road in South Ockendon. Ever the entrepreneur, he was one of the first to dream up the idea of drumming up publicity for his business by organizing bonny-baby competitions through newspapers. The prize was £200. Ron would invite parents to get free portraits of their kids to enter the contest – which was open to all children between the ages of one month and eight years and staged at the Co-op department store in Grays – hoping of course that they would order a set of pictures anyway. Meanwhile Ron, who also judged the event, got several weeks of free publicity in the local paper into the bargain.

So it was fitting that Ron and Barbara's only child – born on 4 June 1975 at Orsett Hospital – would turn out to be an exceptionally beautiful baby, with large wide-set brown eyes, long eyelashes and unusually full lips, still recognizable today. It wasn't long before Russell's angelic features were being used by Ron to advertise his latest contest.

Tellingly, maybe, it was Barbara who registered Russell Edward's birth five weeks after he was born. Prophetically, the name 'Russell' was coming back into fashion that year, thanks to the popularity of a TV presenter with a distinctly camp delivery. In 1975, talk-show host Russell Harty was approaching the peak of his fame as ITV's answer to Michael Parkinson.

Although baby Russell was perfect in every way, instead of bringing his parents together, his birth only laid bare the underlying tensions in Ron and Babs's six-year marriage. Russell was six months old when the couple split. Ron later blamed the stress of working long hours, trying to make a success of his business.

Neighbours recall that it didn't take long for Babs – who had always been a strong independent woman with a career of her own – to realize that perhaps she was better off without him. 'She was a very good mother. You got the feeling she was happy to be mother and father to Russell,' said one, who vividly recalls a heavily pregnant Babs pushing her broken-down car up the hill – while Ron looked on. 'He was *her* son and she wanted to take care of everything. She always coped extremely well. She and Russell were very close from the start.'

After Ron left, he did not see his son again until Russell was walking and talking a year later. It had been an acrimonious separation – and Ron blamed his absence from Russell's life on his tense relationship with Babs.

In the years that followed, Ron did his best to see Russell at weekends, often taking his son to visit his sister Janet and her children. When Russell was five, Ron took him to Upton Park for his first West Ham game. Stunned by the sight of thousands of fans streaming out into Green Street, Russell had looked up and asked Ron if everyone in the world was assembled there. For years afterwards, the shared love of the club was to be a strong bond between father and son – with Russell ringing his dad at half-time to update him on the score.

But there were other instances when Ron would not turn up on time on Saturdays, as promised, and Russell was 'set out in my little coat, waiting for a man who never came'. For the boy, these were the most important dates in the calendar. For Ron, turning up late was no big deal, and he was oblivious to the torments he put his young son through. When he did finally arrive, Ron would shout through the letter box, 'Where's my fucking son?' and then afterwards blame everyone but himself for the fact that Russell was in tears.

As far as Ron was concerned, he had done the right thing getting out of the marriage – claiming it was better to leave than to stay and bicker with Babs in front of their young son. He would maintain it was nothing out of the ordinary – saying a third of marriages break up – and at least Russell had a tranquil home environment with Babs.

Regardless, Russell simply felt rejected. He wanted the picture-postcard family. At times, he felt he would have been happy to live with the rows if it meant having his dad around. In Russell's mind, Ron had deserted him, a 'poor defenceless baby', to pursue his business ambitions – and because he didn't want to deal with a wife and child. Babs finally divorced her husband when Russell was three, citing not one, but two other women as co-respondents.

Russell never got over his resentment against Ron for abandoning him and consigning Babs to bring him up without regular maintenance. The betrayal was to leave a deep and indelible scar. Though Ron loved his son, he was always unable – or unwilling – to face up to the hurt he caused Russell. Ron's own dad had died when he was eight: Ron himself had no role model for a father.

Over the years, Ron's mixed business fortunes meant that

Barbara could not rely on money from her ex-husband. Russell remembers that his mum could be 'volatile', while Ron would be 'abrupt'. It meant that when Ron did turn up, there were frequent rows about money.

Life for a single mother in the seventies was not easy. To support her son, Babs worked at a company in the nearby town of Stanford-le-Hope – and also took jobs on the side selling everything from dishwashers to clothing. Often, it was a constant juggling act to find people who could look after Russell while she worked. Luckily, she had friends in the Close who helped her out. Ron's sister Janet was also not too far away – and Russell would go over to their house for Christmas sometimes and to play with his cousins.

Nevertheless, it was a struggle. Because of the family circumstances, Russell was entitled to free school meals, but Babs still made him sandwiches anyway. While other families went abroad on their holidays, Russell and Babs spent their breaks on caravan sites in Margate or Poole. On one occasion when he lost his trainers, Russell recalled the humiliation of having to go to school in a pink pair belonging to his mum.

Still, whatever their financial fortunes, Babs was determined not to let them show. Whenever she turned up at the school gates, Russell's schoolmates remember she was always perfectly turned out. Other mums may have appeared in tracksuits. But Babs always stood out with her perfect make-up and piled-high bouffant hair which – according to one student – made her look 'like she was going to a job interview'.

Then Ron would be back on the scene. Whenever business was going well, he would try to make his absence up to his son, buying expensive toys or making a grand entrance at his birthday parties. One time, Ron planned to spend some quality time with Russell by taking him away on holiday to Pontin's. Surprisingly, perhaps, Russell, who was seven, never volunteered for the kiddie talent show, instead preferring to while away the hours playing arcade games.

Nonetheless, nothing could make up for the fact that, unlike other children's fathers, his wasn't always around. Russell hated school sports days – not only because he detested P.E., but also because his dad wasn't there to cheer him on. On one such day, when he was supposed to run the return lap in a two-lap race, he ran over to his mum instead. Russell wanted to be a soccer player when he grew up and wished he could live up to his father's prowess as a sportsman. Later, he ruefully observed that Ron was a bit of a show-off with the ball, while he was so bad he would run in the other direction. It was not until Russell was an adult that he was to find a common interest with Ron: women.

Although it is hard to imagine now, Russell was a shy, polite little boy who often stared down at his feet when being spoken to and from whom, at times, it was hard to raise even a 'hello'. As an only child, Russell perhaps internalized some of his feelings of worry and rejection about his parents' split, having no siblings with whom he could discuss or share the trauma. Like many young children of divorce, he believed his dad had left him – not his mother. Often, he would spend long hours gazing in the mirror, talking to himself. The fact that sometimes Ron would be around and then he'd disappear again made it even more confusing and unsettling.

'It was a subject you had to tread around delicately,' recalled his former classmate Claire Honeywell, who was in the same class as Russell at Little Thurrock Primary. 'In those days, most people's parents were still together. I remember the teachers telling us that Russell's mum and dad didn't live together any more, so that we didn't tease him about it. It was quite poignant, really.'

From the outset, Babs felt she could fulfil the role of both parents. From the moment he had opened his eyes, Russell had been her universe and she adored him. She delighted in her son's mischievous sense of humour, his clever way with words. Babs never tired of telling him how handsome he was, or giggling at his jokes.

Even during his worst depths of drug-taking and debauchery in his early twenties, although Babs worried about him and looked out for him – she rarely censured him. She would call him her 'cheeky monkey', and always made sure he had enough money and was eating properly. Russell just loved her all the more for letting him be himself. He would laughingly admit that his mother had 'mollycoddled' him – and that her all-forgiving indulgence had led him to turn out the way he had.

It was clear from the number of pictures of Russell around the house who the most important person in Babs's life was. One of her favourites was a portrait of Russell aged about six, peering from behind a tree. The term 'little angel' could have been invented for him, with his mop top of brown hair, tilted head and huge grin.

Moreover, the affection runs both ways. Throughout his life, his mother's tears have been one of the few restraining influences on Russell. As an adult, not a day goes by when he does not ring her. His loyalty to his mother is so total that when, years later, Babs was upset by some apparently anodyne remarks that Ron made to a newspaper about Russell's childhood, Russell severed all contact with him. And when Bob Geldof called him 'a cunt' at an awards ceremony in 2006, it was the fact that Babs had been hurt by the remark that made Russell most angry. Never mind that 'Do They Know It's Christmas?' had been the first record he'd ever bought, at the age of nine.

As Russell later said of his mother in *GQ*: 'She has been the one constant thing in my life through good and bad. And I love her so much for that. She's a gentle, caring, compassionate, kind, lovely, funny woman.'

Despite his undoubted love for Babs, Russell has admitted he could be a challenging child: 'I gave my mum hell – and she's the one who stayed. She didn't need that kind of aggravation, poor cow. Bless her heart.' At times, Babs had to deal tactfully with her son's sexual precociousness. Well before other children knew about the birds and the bees, Russell was fascinated by the workings of sex and the wonders of the female form. One day, when a well-endowed and attractive female neighbour opposite had problems with her plumbing, she asked Babs if she could have a bath at her house. Russell saw his chance – and set up his Star Wars toy figures in the bathroom. He recalled later: 'I properly fancied her. Mum said I had to get out of the bathroom. But Josie goes: "I don't mind – he's only six. Leave him in here." "You fools," I thought. "I know exactly what I am doing!"'

Already his mind was always working overtime, often dreaming up ways to shock. He once played a most unpleasant trick on Babs to test her reaction. He sprayed the toilet seat with Jif – and then told his mother that his willy had gone hard and made a mess on the toilet seat. He was only eight. It was a difficult moment for any parent: Babs diplomatically responded by telling Russell not to worry – explaining that he was just unusually sexually mature for his age.

Sex wasn't the only area in which he showed an early interest: he was precocious in his fashion sense, too. Even as a child, Russell had a dandyish edge. He remembered how he once asked his mother for a dressing gown with a silk lining, like a dapper Noel Coward.

Despite her best efforts, Babs's unquestioning patience and understanding weren't enough to give Russell a completely happy childhood. He still felt trapped and powerless. 'I had a lot of prohibiting, inhibiting things around,' he recalled later in The Observer. 'My feeling about my childhood was that it was lonely and difficult. Of course,

I've been through lots of therapy. But I do feel a sense of "you poor little sod".'

That feeling was compounded when a new man entered Barbara's life. Colin Clifford had met Barbara at a party when Russell was seven. He worked as a delivery-van driver. A good-looking, well-built man who liked a drink, he later moved in with Babs and continued to live with her until well after Russell left home. Used to having his mum to himself, Russell hated having a rival for Babs's attention. He bitterly resented Colin's macho presence in his house, describing him as an unwelcome intruder, 'just sitting around, drinking Tennant's, dominating the sitting room.' He later observed that like his dad Ron, Colin had once been considered for a place on the West Ham squad. Yet even the shared interest in the club appears to have done nothing to bring them closer. To Russell, it felt like 'another male role model letting me down'.

Nor did Colin seem to want a surrogate son. He had no kids of his own. In interviews, Russell has always referred to Colin as his stepfather. But when approached about his own attitudes to the relationship, Colin makes it plain how he felt. 'I lived with Babs for a few years' is how he describes the relationship. 'I was never a father figure to Russell. I called him Russ and he called me Colin.'

And it quickly becomes clear why – in Colin's own words – the two 'went their separate ways'. He is a bullish man with a forceful presence. While he recognized Russell as 'a very bright talented boy', he probably had little time for the child's more bizarre idiosyncrasies, let alone some of his more weird behaviour. Indeed, Russell later recalled in an interview with *The Word* magazine: 'I felt like he hated me, this flouncy kid. I was all: "Ooh, Noel Coward."'

However, whatever Colin did, it would have been hard to please Russell, who viewed him principally as a competitor for his mother's affections. So Russell remained Barbara's responsibility – even if they were all living under the same roof.

Neighbours felt that Babs was content to bring up Russell herself – and never encouraged Colin to take a fatherly role. Said one: 'She felt she loved him enough for both [parents].' Therefore, it was not surprising that when Babs first got cancer, Russell was terrified of what would happen to him without the most important person in his universe.

Babs first fell ill when Russell was eight. For the next ten years, she fought three different types of cancer: breast, uterine and lymph. According to Colin, it was 'sheer willpower' – and no doubt a determination to stick around for the sake of her son – that pulled her through.

It was to mark the start of a traumatic period for Russell. While Barbara was being treated at the Royal Marsden Hospital in London, he would be sent away to stay with his dad or his grandmother, Jen, in Dagenham, or with Babs's relatives. He just felt lost. 'I didn't like that,' Russell told the *Sunday Herald* later. 'I was not happy in those situations. It's not good for you, for your identity. And it makes you not trust stuff.

'I never felt secure,' he remembered. 'I always had this feeling that she might not be around much longer and then what would I be left with?' Instead, he escaped by immersing himself in TV, and analyzing comedy hits like *Blackadder*, *Fawlty Towers* and *Only Fools and Horses*. As he observed to *The Guardian*, 'Most of my formative relationships were with television and mirrors.'

To give him stability, Russell was sent to Hockerill, a state boarding school in nearby Bishops Stortford. He was eleven and it was his first year of secondary school. But he hated being away from home and missed his mother so much that he came back after a year. As Ron later recalled: 'He was miserable and used to cry to come home.'

Russell's first girlfriend, Melanie Gillingham, who dated him when he was fifteen, recalls what a deep shadow the cancer had cast over Russell. 'I remember that I had a lump on my breast and we were talking about it. He became really worried. He kept saying: "You have to go to the doctors. You have to go and get it checked out." You could tell he was really worried. He was very caring like that.'

Ultimately, the result was that Russell became desperate to be in charge of his own destiny, instead of feeling pushed from pillar to post. His childhood ambition was 'to become chairman of a committee of like-minded children and eventually achieve dominance over the adult world'. It is perhaps no coincidence that when asked at what age he would like to live for the rest of his life, Russell chose seven. 'It was an innocent time when I was unmarred and unsullied – just a lad trying to live life.' Nineteen eighty-two was the year before his mother first had cancer – and she met Colin. To cap it all, Ron also remarried shortly before Russell's eighth birthday. Russell's new stepmother was an air stewardess called Carol. Ron was thirty-nine. Carol was twenty-five.

By his mid-teens, Russell increasingly started to look critically at his own body. Though by no means obese, he had always been quite a chubby child with a cherubic face. When he compared his slightly podgy frame to the athletic builds of his father and Colin, Russell felt fat and weak in comparison. He was too uncoordinated to lose the extra weight on the football pitch. But when he found he could eat, and then vomit it all up again, the sense of control he had over his own body was euphoric. It was also an extraordinary cry for help, considering that bulimia is a condition extremely rare in boys – who usually do not get it until adulthood. It was to be the first of many different obsessions in a lifetime of compulsions.

It didn't help that he'd been bullied about his size by some of the tougher boys. In fact, Russell would later confide to friends that he had been given a hard time because he was so bad at sport; even the egg-and-spoon races at sports days were a trial for him. Russell's self-image was that he was a 'weak little child' and a 'fat little weed'. 'I'd binge and be sick,' he told the *News of the World*. 'I was a fat little kid. I wanted to lose weight and conform to a more recognizable form of masculinity.'

Yet really all Russell wanted was for someone to acknowledge how unhappy he was. Soon, the vomit started to block up the drains in the bathroom sink. But Colin, who no doubt didn't have a clue about the condition before it had been talked about by Diana, Princess of Wales, responded by asking Russell to choose somewhere else to be sick because it was causing havoc with the plumbing.

It was 1987, and Russell had just turned twelve, when he returned from his short-lived spell at boarding school to attend the local comprehensive, Grays School. He had just come through a difficult period, during which he hadn't known whether his mother would live or die. Almost losing Babs meant Russell had subconsciously become aware that he had to seize every moment – and behave almost as if it was his last. The feelings of impotence he had felt as a young child were now turning to anger. He tried cutting the inside of his forearm, to see if making himself bleed would relieve the misery he felt on the inside. It left him with several oval-shaped scars.

'I did feel it was unjust, you know,' he later told the *Sunday Herald*. 'Just growing up with my mum, my stepdad moving in, not getting on with him, and my dad not being there, and not really getting on with men, and my mum getting ill a lot. It was traumatic and lonely and we didn't have no money.'

As a late arrival to the school, Russell was to face a tough time fitting in. An old school friend recalled: 'As far as I knew, it was verbal rather than physical bullying. It was a working-class macho area, so of course Russell stood out. For one thing, he had that slightly effeminate manner, so he had to learn to turn that to his advantage by being funny. Humour was his way of controlling what they said about him.'

Russell was also a target because of his plumpness. English teacher Cheryl Benton recalls: 'It was all puppy fat – he wasn't obese by any means. But he was obviously self-conscious and he got quite a hard time about it from the other kids. Looking back, I think it's possible that being funny was Russell's defence mechanism. His exuberance was a barrier, so that he could make a joke before anyone else could make one at his expense.' In years to come, Russell would tell friends that the teasing he received at school made him even more determined to succeed in later life.

From an early age, Russell had a precocious intelligence, which went hand in hand with a natural gift for language. As an only child, he was an avid reader. He was also blessed with a sharp memory and a talent for collating and cross-referencing information, no matter how bizarre. It meant that even without the benefit of a classical education, Russell always sounded well read. 'I can hear a lot of cultural references, lace them together in my mind and send them back out there,' he explained later.

Even at school, he had his own catchphrases, which he quickly learned to use to comic effect with his friends. Long before he had come up with ''citing' and 'Hang the man who says so', he was experimenting with phrases like: 'Don't do that!' and 'I demand an explanation!'

As a boy, his imagination was captured by film and television. He would later comment that he was 'raised by TV'. Some of his favourite childhood afternoons were spent at the State cinema in Grays, a magnificent art deco 2,000-seater.

Built in 1938, it was a monolith of a movie theatre, with a huge tiered upper circle. It was one of the last remaining classic cinemas in operation in Britain in the eighties. As late as the 1970s, a man would still rise up through the floor, playing a luminous mauve Compton organ. For Russell, going to the cinema was the ultimate escape – and he dreamed of being up there on screen. Throughout his life, he would often make reference to some of the most popular films of his childhood, including the *Indiana Jones*, *Star Wars* and *Back to the Future* trilogies.

A bright child, Russell had started off at school as the kid who always had his hand in the air. But because the classes were mixed ability, he quickly grew frustrated and bored to be taught with kids who were light years behind him. Even aged six, he remembers feeling indignant that he should be in the same class as some of the slower learners.

As he grew up, it dawned on Russell that being the cleverest boy in the class was not going to make him popular. Instead, his mental energy now went into being the class clown. It was as if shouting the loudest at school would blot out the pain, fear and loneliness of a boy who didn't know where he stood in the world.

Not that the teachers were unaware of Russell's intelligence. They just didn't have the time or resources to do anything with it. 'Grays really was a bog-standard comprehensive. No one had much imagination or ambition at all,' recalls Cheryl Benton. 'It was a bit like turning out sausages when you were a teacher at a school like that. It is difficult to cope with someone different and individual. You don't want someone like Russell who stands out and wants lots of attention. If you had put Russell in some really creative public school, he probably would have thrived. But at Grays, Russell was an anomaly.'

There were several other reasons why you couldn't ignore

Russell Brand, who was happy to play the part of the nancy boy if it got him a few laughs. Cheryl remembered: 'He had this aura of confidence around him – but I am not sure that deep down he really felt it. It looked more like a persona he developed. It was obvious Russell was highly intelligent, but you never felt he channelled it as he should have done. He was the comedian probably because there was no status attached to being academic.'

Already Russell's looks were distinctive. He had a sweep of dark straight hair that hung down like curtains on either side of his face. Usually it was gelled flat. He virtually always looked a scruff; the standard school uniform at Grays was black trousers and blazer – Russell lent it his own twist by wearing his clothes, particularly his trousers, too long, while his white shirt was baggy and invariably hanging out. Looking back, some of his contemporaries think it was Russell's effort to customize his uniform and look cool. Others think it was driven by Russell's shyness about his chubby figure.

Fellow pupil Theresa Cross recalled: 'You got the feeling Russell might have been compensating for other areas where he was not that happy. He looks totally different to the way he did because he was so much shorter and chubbier. But even now I would recognize that voice. He wasn't posh, but he always had a put-on posh accent to be funny. He was very clever, but he was always messing around. If he was interested in drama or English, he would concentrate. In any other subject, he would try and distract you because he was bored. He used to make me laugh with his comments, though. He was always doing little characters with funny accents and turning the situation round. He would chat back to the teachers and was always trying to get the last word.'

In the days before Lakeside Shopping Centre opened, there was little for teenage boys to do in the town except ride bikes and get into trouble. For Russell – or Russ, as he preferred his mates to call him – the main after-school activity was hanging around outside McDonald's in Grays town centre. Russell was known as a laugh who could usually be found at the forefront of the most dangerous and corrupting activities.

As a younger child, he had enjoyed riding his BMX bike around the Close, doing Eddie Kidd impersonations with his friends, and playing with his pets – including a dog called Topsey. Psychologists would have a field day with one of Russell's childhood games. He once told his 6 Music listeners that he would call the dog upstairs, where she was forbidden to go – and then kick her back down. Nevertheless, he was devastated when she had to be put down.

When he was fifteen, Russell got into the habit of nipping back home during school lunch breaks to watch pornography with his mates. One particular favourite was *Garage Girls*. The boys called their unofficial porn club 'the Bermuda Triangle' – because as soon as the videos were lent to anyone, they disappeared. It was on one such occasion that Russell had his first puff of weed. On his return to school that afternoon, he enjoyed the sense of detachment it gave him.

Russell was never alone. He always had friends in tow. And just as he would in later life – in the form of Karl Theobald, Matt Morgan and Trevor Lock – Russell liked to have a straight man to bounce off, and to some extent a protector. At school, Russell's best friend was Sam Crooks. 'They were like Tweedledum and Tweedledee,' recalls one classmate. 'You could tell Russell felt more confident, he had more bravado if Sam was around. Sam was the more sensible one of the two.' At one point, the pair had gone around saying they had cut each other's arms – and swapped blood – to become blood brothers. 'No one knew whether they had or not, but it showed a bit of daring imagination that they should even dream up something like that.'

By the time he was sixteen, Russell was also flirting with

the real discipline-case boys in the school, with whom he would go on shoplifting expeditions to the newly opened Lakeside shopping complex, later recalling: 'I was pretty good at it!' At the time, the mall was brand new and crawling with security guards – and it didn't take much for Russell to do something that made them chase him.

The fact was that whenever Russell was around, there was always something outrageous happening. Russell had enjoyed his power to shock from an early age. He first discovered the feeling when, at the age of six, he had found a dying newt. At first, he was bitterly upset. But when it dried out, he was delighted to find he could use its frazzled body to frighten other kids. He found the sensation empowering.

On another occasion, he turned up at school with a huge love bite on his neck and proceeded to show it off, claiming it was from an over-amorous girlfriend. The story was debunked only when one of the other boys in the class revealed Russell had really got it by sticking the nozzle of a vacuum cleaner on to his neck. Russell retold the tale many years later as a love story between himself and Henry the Hoover on both his radio and TV show.

The reason he did crazy things, he later explained, was to escape the boredom of life in the Essex suburbs. 'I had to deal with feeling ordinary, dull, tedious and powerless by trying to subvert those ideas, being anarchic and dangerous ... You feel this burning need to swim against the natural current of your human misery.'

For although he would play 'Jack the lad' at school, he still felt like an outsider. His favourite writers were Oscar Wilde and Alan Bennett, whom he identified as misfits like himself. He would also spend long hours locked away in his room listening to the music of The Smiths. He had fallen in love with the Manchester band, admiring the clever way they used language to glamorize the awkwardness, loneliness and boredom that Russell also felt. It was partly in homage to frontman Morrissey, a committed vegetarian, that Russell stopped eating meat at the age of fourteen.

Somehow, Russell always seemed to escape getting into trouble, though. He once tipped over a desk in an English lesson when the teacher was out of the room. His classmate Steven Honeywell, who was sitting on it at the time, fell forward, injuring his neck and becoming badly winded. Russell still managed to talk his way out of it.

School friend Ricky Doye recalls: 'Russell was too clever for his own good – and he had the gift of the gab. We would always be up to something, whether the teacher was in the room or not. It was just: "Look at us, look at the funny thing we are doing." It would be impersonations, throwing things – anything to relieve the boredom. But we always stopped short of anything that was too bad.'

'Russell was the person in class that if he spoke to you in lessons, you'd be the one to get in trouble – not him,' classmate Claire Honeywell remembers. 'He just had this knack of getting away with most things. Some of the staff thought the sun shone out of him.'

And Russell always had a smart answer. On one occasion, he turned up late for school – and when the teacher asked him why, he responded: 'Well, you see, Miss, there was this big spaceship ...' The room exploded with laughter – but there were times when his classmates were not impressed, when they *all* had to stay behind because of one of Russell's wisecracks.

As he grew in confidence, Russell's aura of invulnerability was boosted by the fact he gave the impression that he owned the school. Even in the classroom, his open body language – often with his feet on the desk or sitting cross-legged – screamed studied insouciance. 'He would rock back on his chair like he was the elite, with sort of lounging-around body language just like he does now,' recalled Claire Honeywell. 'It was this look, which said: "I am better than all of you."'

There was no stopping Russell out of school, either. On a visit to the Thameside Theatre in Grays, actor Gary Wilmot had thrown a bag of crisps at Russell as part of the show. Russell immediately ate one, loudly proclaimed, 'They're stale!' and threw them back, to the amusement of the audience.

Speaking to many of his old classmates, however, it is clear that – just like it does now – Russell's humour got mixed reactions. While some of his peers thought he was hilarious, others felt intimidated by him. Already Russell was all too aware of the power his way with words could have. When he felt like it, he was easily capable of reducing his schoolfellows to tears of frustration when they couldn't respond in kind. Despite the fact he himself had been teased about his weight and lack of sporting prowess, it didn't stop him ribbing other members of his class. 'He would target whatever weakness you had and expand on it,' recalls Clare Sage. 'People found his personality so overpowering, often they had nothing to say back to him.'

Claire Honeywell found herself at the more vicious end of his sense of humour, as she explains: 'Every day we had to wear white ankle socks. Russell would come up to me and say: "Oh, you've got the same socks on today, Claire?" I would say: "No, Russell, it's a different pair." But the next day, he would come back and say exactly the same thing. It went on for six or seven months. I got so desperate, I thought, "Right, Russell Brand – I'll have you" – and even risked turning up to school one day with no socks on at all, but it didn't make any difference. He wasn't satisfied until he got a rise out of me. He was horrible.'

But while Russell didn't mind doling it out, he didn't enjoy getting it back. If his jokes did not go down well, it was a different story. 'If you told him to shut up, he didn't like it much. He'd get a bit sulky,' recalls fellow pupil Theresa Cross. And there was also a quiet, sullen side to Russell. 'He could be a Jekyll and Hyde. One minute, he would be all jokey and laughing. The next minute, he could be moody. He wasn't good at confrontation. He liked people laughing with him, but he didn't like it if you laughed at him.'

Back in the staffroom at Grays Comprehensive – and not for the last time in Russell's academic career – 'What are we going to do with Russell Brand?' was one of the most common topics of conversation. His English teacher Cheryl Benton said: 'All the teachers used to moan about Russell because he just would not do what he was told. But although he could be infuriating, he was incredibly talented with it. I have to admit he made me laugh. He had charm – and he was so grown-up compared with other kids his age. He had a confidence with older people that no one else had.

'People gave him a bit of slack because he wasn't a nasty or malicious kid. He was just exuberant – the kind of child who wouldn't stand in line when you asked him to.'

Drama teacher Colin Hill agrees that Russell's charm usually won the day – whatever he'd been up to. 'You never needed to discipline Russell. He never went quite far enough.'

CHAPTER TWO

'A BLISSFUL EPIPHANY'

*'You might be as famous as me
one day. If so, see you at the top.'*

— RUSSELL, AGE SIXTEEN, ON HIS SCHOOL
GRADUATION AUTOGRAPH CARD

Once every few weeks, Russell's English teacher would give her class a challenge. Dividing the pupils into four groups, she would ask them to improvise around a random situation. Today's subject was a trip to the hairdresser.

For the fourth-year students at Grays School, it was the worst kind of torture. As they reluctantly took turns, most of the class passed the time with exactly the sort of pedestrian observations you would make in a hair salon – holiday destinations or the state of the weather.

In the majority of lessons, you could count on Russell Brand to be skulking at the back of the class, flicking rubber bands, passing notes and generally making a nuisance of himself. But today, Russell was the epitome of enthusiasm. On the spot, he imagined a salon fitted with Dorian Gray-style talking mirrors – and bizarre hairstyles through which clients could communicate with aliens. Finally, after ten minutes of absurdity, he was asked to let someone else have a turn.

Russell Brand was fifteen years old. But already he had an imagination and a way with words well beyond his years. 'It sounded like he had swallowed a thesaurus,' recalls classmate Claire Honeywell. 'We were all awkward adolescents, so for most people, role play was their worst nightmare. But you never had to worry about who would go first with Russell in the lesson. It would be Russell every time – and within about fifteen seconds, the whole thing would be "The Russell Brand

Show". He would go off on all sorts of tangents until the teacher told him to stop.'

With an innate memory for things he had read or heard, Russell instantly stood out for being by far the most articulate boy in his year. 'At fifteen, he was already talking like a twenty-two-year-old,' remembers deputy head Alan Goodwin.

In most ways, Grays School was an ordinary Essex comprehensive. Set in a drab 1932 building, the school was built around a large quad with maths and technology blocks leading off it. Close to a huge council estate, it was a school that had been labelled 'social priority' – which also meant staff got paid more to work there. The results, according to teacher Cheryl Benton, were 'pretty shocking': 'One year, something like only 26 per cent of pupils got five A to C grades, but no one seemed to want to do anything about it. These days, it would be a failing school. There were a lot of poor kids. The area around the school was quite myopic and very inwards-looking. There was nothing middle-class or aspirational about it. Grays was very close to London, but some kids had never been there. A lot of them would end up marrying someone who lived round the corner.'

It meant that stretched teachers had no time to deal with a special case like Russell. When he handed in an English essay in which he had used the words 'grudgingly trudge', he was congratulated on his use of 'resonant language'. Yet time and time again his reports focused not on his exceptional vocabulary, but the fact that Russell spent too much time in class talking.

But though Grays did not excel academically, there was one field where the school was far out in front – drama. Most secondary schools put on a production once a year at the most. Grays School annually staged two major musicals: an old-style music-hall show and a more traditional production. At Christmas, it also put on a pantomime, which played to packed houses every night at the Thameside, the professional theatre in the town. The school was one of the first to offer GCSE drama – and all kids had a compulsory hour of both drama and dance each week.

All this was down to the efforts of head of drama Colin Hill and deputy head Alan Goodwin. The duo were friends who believed that it didn't matter how bright you were – there wasn't a single kid who couldn't gain confidence by performing. They were so passionate, they often appeared in school productions themselves – usually as pantomime dames in the Christmas shows. Russell could not have had a better pair of instructors. When Colin retired from teaching not too long afterwards, he carved out a career as a successful actor in his own right, appearing in Martin Scorsese's *Gangs of New York* with Daniel Day-Lewis and the TV series of *Lock, Stock and Two Smoking Barrels*. Alan also stayed committed to the theatre, and now runs the Canterbury branch of the Stagecoach Theatre Arts School.

Until his fifth year at Grays, Russell had been content to take a back seat – and had never auditioned for any roles in the productions, even though almost everyone who tried out was guaranteed a part of some sort. But now he was facing a crossroads. Making his classmates laugh was all very well, but he had to start thinking about what he was going to do after school. If he didn't want to end up at the local sixth-form college – or in a dead-end job with no qualifications – he was going to have to find something more interesting to do. He had also seen his mother face cancer – now he was in a rush to make his own life count, before it was too late.

So when the posters went up advertising try-outs for *Bugsy Malone*, Russell decided to audition. The Alan Parker children's musical is set in 1920s Chicago. It is an entertaining pastiche of the conventions of the American gangster movie, using splurge guns that fire cream instead of bullets.

In 1976, it had launched the careers of Jodie Foster as Tallulah and Scott Baio as Bugsy. The story went that when looking for a boy to play Fat Sam in the movie, director Alan Parker went to a Brooklyn classroom and asked who the naughtiest boy in school was. All the class replied, 'John Cassisi,' who subsequently got the part. If the casting had been done by the same method at Grays School in 1990, 'Russell Brand' might have been the answer. But unlike John Cassisi, who was virtually never heard of again, this was the role that was to confirm to Russell that acting was his future.

'Russell turned up at the audition completely out of the blue,' remembers Alan Goodwin. 'I think he had realized that the leading lights of the school were in drama and maybe he wanted to be a part of that. Until then, Russell had never come to my attention.'

As Alan auditioned him, it was clear that Russell had something a bit different about him. 'Russell already had flair and a bit of an individual persona. We asked him to audition in a Chicago accent and he more than held his own against the other children who were up for it.'

Russell landed the part of Fat Sam, owner of The Grand Slam Speakeasy. The role required someone who was physically big – and thanks to his remaining puppy fat, Russell just about fitted the bill. As he was still stocky, all that was needed was some padding in the stomach area of his brown pinstriped suit. His voice had not yet broken, but he had a decent singing voice and liked doing physical comedy. With his slicked-back hair and eyeliner moustache, Russell looked like an embryo Clark Gable.

'Russell came to drama fairly late on,' agrees Colin Hill, who was remembered as a hard taskmaster who expected professional standards from his cast – and was not afraid to shout and scream in rehearsals to get the best performances. 'He was a striking boy. As time went on, I think he realized that he could use his natural enthusiasm in the theatrical sense. He stood out, he was a personality.

'He was always very sure of himself, larger than life, even then. He was the kind of person who would run at the wall until the wall fell over. In many ways, he was just Russell. He was playing himself, although funnily enough I would not say he was the best thing in *Bugsy*. But he had the gift of delivery and he was an articulate boy who was able to express himself. He always had an ear for the right words and an amazing ability to manipulate language.'

He adds: 'He was a boy who wanted to be an individual. He had no interest in following the mould. He wanted to go his own way and always got his point across. He could give the impression of being full of himself, but that was sheer overconfidence in the use of his vocabulary.'

Although it was not always to be the case in later life, Russell attended every rehearsal of his first production, knew his lines perfectly and relished his scenes as the hard-edged, hard-talking gangster boss. Recalls Alan Goodwin: 'It was as though Russell was saying: "I am doing my little section now, so watch out, this will be good." You put him under the spotlight and, all of a sudden, he blossomed. It gave him even more confidence to express what he had to say.'

Suddenly, the naturally flamboyant part of Russell's character had free rein. Indeed, a video of the school production shows Russell throwing himself wholeheartedly into the role – although often doing his own thing. With Russell yet to reach his full height, and without a trace of stubble in sight, he is still very much a boy rather than a man. His voice is high, and his hands are out of proportion to his body. One of the main features of his performance are his expansive, even grandiose gestures.

It is a rich comic performance – if at times lacking in concentration. Ten minutes in, Russell breaks one of the first rules of comedy by bursting into a fit of giggles when he gets sprayed with a soda fountain. But it is clear that he already had a good ear, making a convincing stab at an American gangster accent – unlike some of his peers, who were happy to deliver lines in broad cockney. In the finale, where the cast is assembled together, Russell gets bored and wanders off to speak to someone else at the other end of the stage.

Looking at the production now on a shaky videotape, it is hard to see it as anything else but a good-quality school production of an amateur classic. But for Russell, the experience was nothing more than a revelation. Or as he later described it: 'A blissful epiphany.' It was as if, standing between the crimson velvet curtains of Grays' school hall, he had suddenly received a vision of what he was going to do with his life.

In many ways, the production was also an early indicator of what later made him tick as a comedian. At one point, Russell forgot his lines. But instead of panicking, he later recalled that he found the experience exhilarating. 'I had to improvise my way out of it. I felt this sudden rush of adrenalin surging through me. It was like a drug.' It was a heady feeling of risk he was to seek again and again as a stand-up comedian.

Despite his confident performance, however, Russell had been physically sick before he went on. But he did three nights. When he came off stage, he announced to his father that he had finally found his vocation. '"This is what I want to do," he told me,' Ron explained.

There were forgotten lines and stifled giggles. Yet there was a definite spark of something. As Melanie Gillingham, who shared several scenes with him, remembers: 'Technically he made mistakes – he kept turning his back to the audience for one thing – but he had presence.'

Russell had finally found the validation he needed in life.

'He was looking for people to like him,' says Colin Hill. 'In real life, if you are funny, people laugh, but you don't get the applause. If you are funny and on stage, people laugh – and you do get the applause.'

It was also a sign of things to come that some of the girls in his year – those who didn't find him intensely irritating – started to return his interest. The puppy fat was dropping off and he chopped off his lank locks in favour of a Morrissey-style quiff, in honour of his favourite band, The Smiths.

The new look suited him, accentuating his emerging cheekbones, even if he did need a pot of gel to keep it in place. At the time, he was a keen fan of white rapper Vanilla Ice. Seeing an opportunity to imitate his idol, he cut some blonde hair off his dad's girlfriend's lapdog and gelled it into his quiff to give himself ready-made highlights. He completed the image change with a black leather jacket and a louche James Dean-style slouch. Yet Russell was later to claim that as a teenager he was 'insecure' about his looks. It didn't seem to matter to the girls.

'Russell worked his way around the year,' recalled one classmate. 'He always had a different girlfriend. They didn't last long, though. He normally went for the real stunners with perfect figures. And big chests – for their age, anyway.' It was to be a predilection he would carry through to adulthood.

His first serious girlfriend was Melanie Gillingham, who was his leading lady in the school production, *Bugsy Malone*. She recalls that Russell was somewhat tentative when it came to romance at that point. 'It was all very innocent at that stage. I remember going to the cinema with him to see *Who Framed Roger Rabbit?* and him nibbling my nose.'

In fact, Russell's most important early experience with girls was on holiday when he had just turned sixteen. Flush with cash from his latest business venture, Ron took Russell on a luxury trip to Hong Kong, Singapore and Thailand. Even though Russell was barely out of school, Ron actively encouraged his son to get some experience under his belt. Russell had already had one faltering affair. After a night out in Hong Kong, Ron brought back three prostitutes to their hotel room, so that Russell could get a full initiation.

While Ron got down to business with two of the women in the other bed, Russell was enjoying the attentions of a Filipino girl. After awkward sex with her at around 4 a.m., they shared a moment together looking out over the Hong Kong skyline. She sweetly told Russell she would have to leave before she fell in love with him. Overhearing the remark, Ron exclaimed from the other side of the room: 'Oh, bleeding hell! I am going to be sick!'

The next morning, Ron casually looked up from his newspaper and asked if his teenage son had used a condom. When Russell said he hadn't, Ron's only response was to bark gruffly, 'Well, you should have,' before returning to his reading.

In anyone's books, Ron's conduct as a father had been inappropriate. Yet it was one of the few ways Ron knew to reconnect with his son. On the flight home, Ron proudly remarked: 'I went away with a boy. But I am coming back with a man.' For his part, Russell couldn't wait to get back to Grays to tell his mates all about it.

Now the Brands' shared interest in women was to become their bond. Effeminate in manner and useless on the sports field, Russell was only too glad to have some other way of winning his dad's approval. Combined with a naturally high sex drive, it was to lead to a psychological sex addiction that would prove tougher to break than one to hard drugs. As Russell later admitted: 'We got on that vibe together. That's what we do. It's something we can do effortlessly and without really compromising ourselves.'

Back at school, even with just one dramatic role under his

belt, there were ominous signs that Russell's initial success on stage was going to his head. Already he was telling his classmates that stardom was awaiting him – and it was his ticket out of Grays. 'He said that he would be a household name by the time he was twenty. He used to say it so often, we stopped listening. He said he was going to be a Hollywood star,' recalls Melanie. He even committed his grand schemes down on paper, signing his farewell autograph card to her with the words: 'You might be as famous as me one day. If so, see you at the top. Love, Russ.'

Indeed, Russell was already working on how he could turn drama into his career. A couple of older pupils from the school had landed parts in *Grange Hill* – then the most popular kids' TV programme – and Russell could definitely see himself on the show. He wasted no time signing up to an extras agency to get some walk-on roles.

Impressed by Russell's *Bugsy* performance and recognizing that drama was a natural outlet for their son's exuberance, both Ron and Barbara were firmly behind him. Further drama training seemed the next obvious step. Italia Conti, an established performing-arts school, offered a one-year foundation course. Based on the edge of the City, close to the Barbican, the college was famous for grooming legions of young performers on to stage and television.

In preparation for his upcoming audition, Russell got some publicity shots taken. Many of them were moody James Dean-type poses. In others, he stares up at the camera with what can only be described as a scowl.

In the meantime, for Russell's follow-up role, Colin and Alan had rewarded the aspiring star with a part in the Christmas pantomime, which they felt would make the most of his natural comic talent. Russell was cast as one half of the farcical duo Hammer and Tongs in *Cinderella*.

But, in his mind at least, Russell had already moved on. He

rarely turned up at rehearsals – and when he did, he hadn't learned his lines. It was as if he felt he didn't need the part. Greatness was already beckoning. Finally, Colin and Alan lost patience with him – and sacked him from the role. It would not be for the last time.

'Russell was cocky,' recalled Melanie. 'He thought he was king of the stage after *Bugsy*. He decided that was it. He was going to be an ACT-OR – and he got a little bit pretentious. He didn't even seem to mind when he got sacked from the pantomime. It was as if nothing was going to get in his way.'

Eventually, Russell left school with just four GCSEs: Bs in English Language, Literature and Drama – and a C in History. With fame just around the corner, he didn't particularly appear to care that he had failed all the rest.

It seemed like he had been gone only a short while when Colin Hill opened up the *Thurrock Gazette* and found that Russell was now tipping himself for stardom in the press. His ambition, the budding actor modestly added, was to be 'a movie star'.

'There was Russell with a big grin, practically saying he had already made it. The truth is it took him fifteen years. He just announced it earlier than everyone else.'

CHAPTER THREE

TRAINING FOR THE TOP

*'Other students had to be
spoon-fed. Russell would just
throw the spoon away.'*

The entrance hall of the Italia Conti Academy is a tribute to its former students. From great British entertainment legends like Noel Coward, through to Gertrude Lawrence and Leslie Phillips, the walls are lined with portraits of the show-business names that have passed through its halls. Founded in 1911, the Academy is one of the oldest stage schools in the world. Famous for giving youngsters the best possible preparation for a life in show business, it is also the only school to offer full-time courses in acting, dancing and singing, as well as a formal education.

Most teenagers with not much more than a supporting role in a school play under their belt might have been intimidated. But most teenagers weren't like Russell Brand.

Certainly, Russell's audition pieces had been ambitious. In front of a panel of judges, Russell gave a stirring performance of Lorenzo's speech from Shakespeare's *The Merchant of Venice*. He spoke clearly and gave the speech some original twists. His second attempt was a more daring – and ultimately less successful – choice. Russell launched into a speech from *Confusions*. Aptly named, it was taken from a series of five one-act plays by Alan Ayckbourn, in which five actors play twenty characters to show the many facets of human nature. Russell chose a speech by philandering travelling salesman, Harry. It didn't go down well, but he still got marks for trying. In Russell's audition notes, the verdict was that he had made 'the wrong choice – but at least he was making an attempt'.

Overall, the reviews on Russell's audition were mixed. While Russell had only a 'reasonable' voice, there was raw talent, confidence and a stage presence, and it was felt that he would 'benefit from training'. He was offered a place on the one-year course, on condition that he gave up his work with his extras agency.

Drama school was an expensive proposition, though. Back then, the fees were £1,700 a term – a substantial sum in 1992. Ron had now moved out of the photography business. Currently, he was a national marketing director for a firm selling water filters. It was good money – and he was 100 per cent behind Russell's dreams of becoming an actor.

When his second marriage had broken up, Ron had moved back in with his mum Jen in Lillechurch Road, Dagenham. When he married for the third time in 1991, to a sales coordinator called Rachel (this time seventeen years his junior), Russell was a witness.

With Babs still dealing with her third bout of cancer, Russell had mixed feelings about leaving home. Yet he found seeing his mother with a man he detested as intensely as Colin upsetting. Russell found his macho presence oppressive – and the two clashed repeatedly. 'It was a classic case of two Alpha males in the same house,' recalled one friend. 'He couldn't stand being around Colin any longer.' First Russell moved in with Ron at his new flat in Brentwood; and then in with Jen, taking the District Line tube every morning to the Barbican.

In atmosphere, Italia Conti was close to the sort of stage school depicted in *Fame*. The walls were lined with posters from the great movies and stage shows. The whole place screamed exuberance. Kids thought nothing of tap-dancing in the corridors or singing at the tops of their voices on the staircases. Russell was in his element. As he later told *The*

Daily Telegraph: 'I loved it because it was the point of departure from feeling all fat and unattractive and peculiar in Grays.'

Liberated from the need to conform, he was also already working on creating his own unique image. His year group was spared from wearing the blue school uniform. But there was a dress code. Diploma students were still required to wear 'blacks' – nondescript black tops and trousers – so they could turn their hand to anything from stage management to sword-fighting lessons.

More often than not, Russell infuriated his teachers by wearing whatever he felt like. This included a long coat he named 'the Cape of Love', which he used as part of his chat-up of the various attractive young girls who attended the college, who at the time included stars-in-waiting Martine McCutcheon and Louise Nurding – neither of whom succumbed to his charms.

In an interview with *The Observer*, Russell has since said he was asked to leave Italia Conti 'for smashing things up, crying and cutting myself, breaking down in tears all the time'. But according to Ron Brand, the reason wasn't quite so dramatic: 'I wouldn't say he was expelled. I went to see them after his first year and they said it was best if he didn't go back.'

While Russell was a long way from being a model student, certainly there is nothing in the college records to show that he was kicked out. Instead, Russell's main problem was that he rarely showed his face. The new-found freedom meant that he bothered to attend only the subjects he liked.

And just as he had at Grays School, Russell was soon driving his teachers to distraction. You can almost hear the hair being pulled out in Russell's reports. Elocution teacher Linda James called Russell: 'an intellectual boy with a charming manner.' But charm alone, she added, was not enough to compensate for Russell's 'sheer laziness and apathy'. When he did make an appearance, she found that he had failed to prepare set pieces. As for dialect lessons, Linda found it impossible to comment at all, saying she had seen Russell only once in the entire year.

It was a similar verdict from his acting teacher, Kenneth Michaels, who also commended Russell's 'intelligence, wit and a good sense of fun'. But on the downside, he said Russell was not a team player – an essential requirement for a career in the theatre. What's more, Russell constantly interrupted other students by talking in class. Urging Russell to concentrate more, he signed off by saying: 'He should forget about mirrors in acting class and needless distractions.'

There were yet more 'unexplained absences' from script-reading classes. Although, on the plus side, Russell 'shows enthusiasm and a sense of style in his reading. He has a sense of timing, but needs to increase the range of his voice and his fluency.'

From an early age, Russell had never been the most coordinated boy. So it is perhaps no surprise there were no plaudits for him when it came to stage fighting. In fact, his teacher Philip Stafford's report reads like a stream of anguished frustration: 'Must gain some control in movement, including timing, balance, coordination, interaction – and above all judgement. Single sword is weak. Rapier and dagger is confused. Must place his feet, legs, hands and arms in the mechanically necessary aspects to his partner to make the patterns of movements actually work. Unarmed occasionally effective. Theatrical ability limited. One has to appear to be a person of style, skill and technical strength. Even the simplest unarmed moves must be made with accuracy and authority.'

To his relief, Russell was spared more singing training because his voice was still breaking. But even when he did attend, Russell usually hoped to wing it rather than put in any practice. 'Russell is lucky in having a good basic voice supported by good breathing, but his concentration is poor,' read his music report. 'I would like him to understand that voice work must be based on sound technique – and not luck.'

Yet it was a totally different story if Russell loved a subject. You could not keep him away. And when it came to his improvisation reports, it was as if his teachers were talking about a different boy.

Once a week, the class would meet for an hour and a half in the studio in the basement. Taught by a brave and inspired teacher called Denis Noonan, students were encouraged to let their minds wander wherever they felt like. In the early classes, Denis would bring in kids' toys to encourage his pupils to be as uninhibited as they had been when they were children.

The main exercises were improvisation sessions called 'freeze and change'. Students would be given a scenario to act out and then have to add to it by ad-libbing new plot lines. There was no right or wrong – and it didn't matter if the sketch didn't work. The important thing was to give ideas free rein.

Just as it had been at Grays, it was the one subject where Russell excelled. 'He followed his imagination wherever he went,' recalls Denis. 'Other people just couldn't keep up with him. They would stop because they got scared of where they were going – and one by one they would drop out. It was very rare that anyone could go the distance with Russell because he outpaced everyone else. It was almost like a stream of consciousness. Nothing fazed him.

'With most people, you had to give them the ball. Russell took the ball and ran off with it. He might pass the ball to you for two seconds, but then he would be screaming for it back again. He never ran out of ideas. He enjoyed the fact that it was a totally blank canvas.

'I remember once asking the students to imagine they were in a doctor's waiting room. Russell played it as if he were inside a human being and bumping into the lungs and the heart and the other organs. It was absurd, but he got there logically – and it still made total sense. Sometimes, Russell could go on for a full twenty minutes. It would be fascinating to see how far he could go. You'd think he'd come to the end of the line, but his mind was so clear that he could find another idea. Other people had to be spoon-fed. Russell would just throw the spoon away.'

Russell loved the fact that whatever he said or did in the class, Denis was totally unshockable. However much his student ranted and swore, Denis never batted an eyelid. 'Afterwards, I would say: "Interesting, Russell. I wouldn't like to live with you in your head, but you are obviously comfortable with it." Occasionally, I would have to remind him: "Remember you have an audience – or else it's nothing more than wanking." Russell would just say: "Well, I enjoy wanking!" There wasn't a niche for Russell, so he made one. I remember telling him: "If you don't fit anywhere, you become unique. We are all unique if it comes from ourselves." ' It was advice Russell was to take to heart.

Overall, Russell's year at Italia Conti had not been a resounding success – and few of the staff were sorry to see him go. Ultimately, it was Russell's stage-production teacher Bonnie Lithgoe who summed it up, when she wrote to his parents: 'What can I say about Russell that won't upset you? Really, not a lot. I am afraid he has wasted his year at the Academy. He has been to several of my classes, but never dressed correctly. And frankly, I am fed up with telling him. He puts very little effort into his work.'

Yet leaving under a cloud wasn't enough to dent his confidence. Denis recalled, just as his school drama teacher Colin Hill had: 'If you had told Russell he was fucking awful, he wouldn't have believed you. He had too much self-belief.'

Indeed, Russell had a TV role lined up. Through being

signed up with an extras agency, he had already made a brief appearance in *Rides* – a short-lived kids' BBC TV series starring Lucy Speed. Now, he had been offered an audition for *Mud* – a seven-part BBC TV show, which went out on Thursday afternoons at 4.30. The plot revolved around the clashes between two gangs of kids aged between ten and fourteen at an adventure holiday camp. One was a group of inner-city kids, the other a group of well-off children.

Russell won the part of Shane, an older camp counsellor whose job it was to break up the fights. The role called on him to spend most of the time sneaking off into the bushes to kiss his fellow camp counsellor, played by a pretty young actress called Paloma Baeza.

Russell couldn't believe his luck – and he wasted no time in trumpeting his success in his local newspaper, the *Thurrock Gazette*, which proudly proclaimed: 'Russell gets his big TV break.'

The series was shot over three particularly freezing months at the end of 1993 at a scout camp in Chalfont St Giles. It was a hard-going shoot involving a lot of wading through mud, and waterproof clothing. The cast lived together in huts dotted about the scout camp. As one of the oldest on the show, Russell, now eighteen, found to his delight that a lot of the younger members of the cast looked up to him as 'a real actor'.

An appearance in *The Bill* is almost a rite of passage for a young thespian – and Russell felt like he was on a roll when he also landed a part in the long-running police drama. The episode, called *Land of the Blind*, was broadcast in October 1994. His character was a young tearaway called Billy Case. It was a morally complex episode, in which a young thug is arrested for beating up and nearly blinding a black man on an estate in a vicious racist attack. The wife of the victim, Mrs Kerr, names Billy as the only assailant. She is able to identify him because she once taught him at school. In fact, Billy's friends were also present – but he refuses to say there were other people involved in order to protect his mates.

Mrs Kerr hides the fact that Billy was only a witness to the beating. Because she would not be able to identify the real culprits positively, she would rather have Billy falsely convicted to set an example. Eventually, DS Deakin spots the inconsistencies in her story. Mrs Kerr is furious, as she is forced to admit that she didn't tell the full truth, and that she was prepared to lie in court to fit up an innocent boy.

In the opening scene, police storm Billy's home to arrest him. He is then interviewed by the cops – and put in a prison cell for an emotional confrontation with his mum, in which he confesses he is covering up for his cronies. Finally, he is seen being led away from court, throwing his mother an imploring look.

Dressed in a hoodie, with an earring and the first hint of sideburns, Russell is almost physically unrecognizable. In all, Russell had no more than twenty lines, including: 'I don't believe this is happening', 'I got the right to a solicitor, ain't I?' and 'I never did any of that!' But it is a very natural performance, in which he veered effortlessly between gormlessness, thuggish bravado and apprehension about what will happen to him if he does not tell the truth. Intrinsically, it was not a sympathetic part. Yet Russell brought enough subtlety to the role to make viewers feel sorry for him.

Despite his strong acting, there was no further work in the offing. But Russell's previous brushes with real life had proved to him once and for all that the last thing he wanted to do was get a 'proper job'.

One Christmas, he had taken a temporary job as a postman near his mum's home in Grays. Unaware that there was a postal strike, Russell thought it would be an easy bit of extra cash. During his round, he stopped to watch an amateur football match. When the ball went out of bounds and he kicked it back, one of the players noticed Russell's postbag. Suddenly, Russell found himself surrounded by the very postmen whose job he was currently doing. To keep their spirits up during the strike, they had been passing the time with a game of soccer. Now they were none too impressed to find a member of the scab labour force watching their game. As he was besieged by enraged posties calling him 'a fucking scab', Russell weakly protested it was Christmas. It was a hard lesson in trade-union politics. The bright side, however, was that Russell nicked a load of mail-order CDs and 'saved a fortune on Christmas presents'. The incident came back to haunt him years later, after he admitted the thefts in an article – and a resident made a complaint to the police. When the dates didn't correspond, Russell was let off.

In the months after he left Italia Conti, Russell was plunged into despair. Ex-girlfriend Melanie Gillingham recalled: 'I bumped into him in Lakeside around that time. His hair was longer. We had a chat and he was a bit low because things weren't taking off for him.' Russell recalled later: 'I can be miserable as fuck. When I was younger, I had difficulties with mental illness, and I was on medication for mood balancing and whatnot. You don't want to be around when the laughter stops.'

Russell's depression was serious enough for him to see a doctor. He was suspected to be bipolar and prescribed Prozac. The analysis explained a lot about Russell's personality – the moodiness; the way he was easily distracted; his impulsive, devil-may-care behaviour; as well as his sexual precociousness. Later, he would also be prescribed Ritalin, but found it made him unable to express himself. For someone as articulate as Russell, it was torture. 'I'd think "I need that word" and I was groping around in the attic for it. Horrible.'

Stardom had not fallen into his lap as easily as he had

hoped. There was only one thing for it – to get some more acting training.

The Drama Centre was set in the decaying buildings hidden behind the handsome façade of a magnificent Grade Two-listed Methodist church on Prince of Wales Road, Chalk Farm, north London. Established in 1963, it was set up to give theatrical training to individuals from working-class backgrounds.

The founder and director was Edinburgh-born Christopher Fettes, a formidable Scot once described as theatre's most notorious outsider. Fettes was also the man Pierce Brosnan called his mentor, after he spotted his talent and accepted him to the school in 1974. Other actors to have learned their craft there are Colin Firth, Frances de la Tour and Simon Callow. More recent graduates have included Tara Fitzgerald, Helen McCrory and John Simm.

Competition was fierce. Every year, 400 students applied in the hope of getting one of the thirty places on offer. The only easy thing about it was the cheap audition fee. After that, the panel of seven judges was looking not just for actors who could play a part, but also for: 'Strength, agility, grace, stamina and courage – the qualities you associate with an athlete.' Whatever Russell had, he certainly had courage.

The fees were £5,250 a year, and a further £3,000 was needed for living expenses. Russell managed to swing a scholarship from a charity that gave grants to young people from poor families who wanted to train in the theatre. Most of the funds, though, he later admitted, were 'squandered on narcotics'. So for a time he lived above a pub and worked shifts behind the bar to help pay the rent.

At the end of the night, Russell would drink up the slops. It was after one such evening that he ended up in a girl's bedsit. He went to the loo in the middle of the night and was so drunk that he wandered into the wrong room on his return.

He claimed he woke up in the morning to find himself in bed with a family of refugees.

'I thought of student life as pressing the pause button on real life,' he later recalled in the *NME Student Guide*, adding that it had taken him three months to learn how to use the Breville toaster. 'I spent the first years of my [student] life eating things that I found emerging from my own body. There's an awful lot you can do with earwax, toenails and a couple of artichokes if you have a creative mind. I didn't buy so much as one textbook in the entire time I was there, but learned from photocopies.'

The regime at Drama Centre was so tough it was nicknamed the Trauma Centre. It was said that if you could survive, you could weather anything your acting career could throw at you. Successful graduates had a reputation among casting directors for being extremely resilient and very focused.

Training was based on the method school. The idea was to try to experience all sensations as the character would. Students were also expected to explore their own personalities and motivations. There were even psychotherapists and counsellors on hand for students who found all the soul-searching too much. Even so, there was a high dropout rate. At the end of each year, up to six students would be asked to leave – either because they couldn't deal with the gruelling regime, or because it was felt they had no realistic hope of a future in acting.

The method was perfect for someone as searingly honest and open as Russell. His most influential drama teacher was the late Reuven Adiv, an assistant to Lee Strasberg in New York. Strasberg was the godfather of modern acting who, in his time, had trained some of the most famous actors of the twentieth century, including Paul Newman, Al Pacino, James Dean, Dustin Hoffman, Marilyn Monroe and Robert De Niro.

At the same time, Drama Centre was also a crash course in dramatic literature. Russell had to read all the classics – from

Aeschylus to Brecht. The workload was intense. Luckily, Russell was a voracious reader. For the first time in his life, he was being intellectually stretched.

By now, Russell certainly had the looks to be leading-man material. His quiff had grown out and he was letting his hair grow. He was also working on his sideburns, which were to become an important part of his look. His *Spotlight* picture at the age of nineteen shows an aggressively handsome, sensuous-looking young man. It was a more self-assured portrait than his earlier mean-and-moody publicity shots.

It seems strange, then, that during this time, one of Russell's sexual conquests, allegedly, was not an equally youthful and blushing teenage beauty, but a seasoned sixty-one-year-old woman. Though he was already getting himself a reputation as a prolific womanizer, this was a claim to notoriety even by Russell's standards. After apparently pulling off the deed, he proceeded to describe the incident to friends in harrowing detail.

At the time, one of his best mates was Jamie Sives, a former scaffolder from Leith in Edinburgh. Jamie had originally decided to go to drama school because he was bored; he was later to find acclaim as the title character in the film *Wilbur*. Russell's other close friend was Karl Theobald, a gangly comic actor six years his senior, who was also later to find success, playing Dr Martin Dear in the TV comedy series *The Green Wing*.

Because Drama Centre was such a small school, it was like joining a theatre company. From the outset, the importance of discipline and timekeeping was drummed into the students. The tone was set on the opening day, when Christopher Fettes announced: 'I don't care if you fuck men, women, dogs or cats, just be here at nine o'clock in the morning.' If students turned up so much as ten minutes late for a class, they would be sent home.

For once, Russell applied himself. He threw himself into his drama reading. An important part of the first year was the Stanislavski Exercises. Stanislavski was a late-nineteenth-century Russian director who had originally pioneered method acting. For the classes, Russell had to imagine the plays as if he was living them, improvising events that weren't in the script and searching his memory for experiences and emotions similar to the character's. He excelled so much that his nickname was 'golden boy'.

'Russell was a brilliant character actor with a marvellous sense of humour,' Christopher Fettes recalls. 'He was very imaginative and was always doing very daring, unexpected things which were quite off the beaten track. He was never dependent on clichés. When it came to performances, he frequently came up with something absolutely delightful – very, very entertaining – and sometimes quite bold.

'I don't ever remember him being difficult. He was a slightly controversial character and in some ways a bit of a loner, but I think people were genuinely very fond of him. He was always great fun. Had it been a degree course at the time, Russell would have got a first – or at least a very good second.'

Another former teacher was not quite so convinced of Russell's popularity, however. 'He could be flirtatious and cheeky with staff, making inappropriate remarks,' the lecturer said. 'He upset many people, but he got away with it because he was so very talented and original and sparky. I was always sticking up for him because I felt he had talent. A lot of the other teachers would have been happy to see the back of him, though. [I felt] his imagination made him a joy to work with.'

Certainly, Russell took roles to their most eccentric extremes. He bought a mouse in a pet shop and encouraged it to live in his hair, because he thought it would add to the character he was portraying. Even though he was only playing a supporting role, Russell's part in *Arden of Faversham* – an Elizabethan play about a husband who murders his wife and her lover – was deemed a triumph. Russell was 'totally believable and brilliantly amusing'. Says Christopher Fettes: 'He was very funny – but also highly individual. It was one of those performances where you knew there was no other actor on the English stage who could have come up with something like that.'

In another production, Russell played an elderly retired general in the play *Even a Wise Man Stumbles*, a drama by the nineteenth-century Russian playwright Alexander Ostrovsky. Even now, it stands out in Christopher Fettes's mind as one of the most original interpretations he had ever seen.

A contemporary of Russell's is more measured in his assessment. 'It wasn't as if Russell was the next Marlon Brando or anything. It was more that he showed more courage than anyone else. He was a bit wild, but he must have played the game to have lasted more than two years there. It did help, though, if you were a good-looking boy like Russell was.'

There was one part of the course in particular that Russell dreaded – classical ballet and movement classes. They were compulsory. Even for someone usually as unselfconscious as Russell, jumping around the room in a pair of black ballet tights was an ordeal. Teachers recall that, at 6ft 2ins, he cut 'an ungainly figure'. So Russell tried to overcome his embarrassment by turning up to the class drunk. He would then stun his fellow pupils with his highly individual interpretations, often performing in the nude. But his instructor, an elderly Swede named Yat Malgram, who had the inscrutability of a Yoda figure, would scarcely raise an eyebrow, calling them 'most interesting'. Increasingly, drink and drugs were starting to divorce Russell not only from reality – but also his responsibilities.

Russell had started smoking pot with his Grays school friends at the age of fifteen. From that point on, Russell took some kind of drug almost every day. It was not long before he was smoking grass in front of his family – and experimenting to find a drug that would numb the pain he was left with from his childhood.

At midnight, after a day at Drama Centre, he would hop on the tube's Northern Line to go to his grandmother Jen's house in Barking. While she cooked him an omelette, Russell would openly roll a couple of joints. When his nan smelt the smoke, she would ask him: 'They aren't funny cigarettes, are they, Russell? I was watching *Kilroy* the other morning and they said it leads to worse things.'

Ever after, Russell referred to it as his nan's *Kilroy* warning. 'Of course, I scoffed at her for falling for such obvious media scare tactics and then promptly descended into the helter-skelter [of hard drugs].'

Just as Jen had predicted, marijuana was the start of a journey that was to lead him to acid, pills, amphetamines – and ultimately heroin. Many of them made him feel ill. Speed made him nauseous. Crack made him feel like he was 'breathing through plastic'. But even so: 'I thought I felt better with it than without it.'

It was when he found heroin that he found his drug of choice. He first tried it, aged nineteen, at Hackney Central station. Spotting a group of Turkish lads who were smoking heroin joints, he approached and they sold Russell some at a cheap rate. He did not try it again for another year – and his heroin addiction did not kick in until his mid-twenties. But he felt that he had finally found a drug that numbed him. Afterwards, he recalled to *GQ*: 'I went home and smoked and suddenly felt enveloped in a womb of comfort.

'Cannabis was boring, cocaine was titillating for a while, LSD was wonderful and enlightening, but none of them really stopped the pain or reached out to my consciousness in the way that heroin did.'

'Finding heroin, it's like God, home, a lover,' he added to Barbara Ellen in *The Observer*. 'Just this feeling of being engulfed by warmth, everything moving away, your life, everything, and withdrawing into this beautiful sanctuary.'

It was about this time that Russell got his first and only conviction. He was fined £80 for possession of a small amount of marijuana at Grays Magistrates Court. Although, in later life, much was to be made of Russell's colourful arrest record – he later claimed to have been arrested eleven times – his only police record was for carrying a minimal amount of pot.

For Russell, however, his main intoxicant was alcohol. One friend and contemporary recalled: 'Russell was an alcoholic. He was a fucking madman. I had heard about Russell about a year before I met him. When I did meet him, I thought, "Who is this guy?" He was like a throwback to this old Dickens novel, like a Victorian spiv. He could regale you for hours with his great use of language and diction and vocabulary. He was amazing.

'He used to cut himself for any excuse – with pint glasses, razors. He wanted to be Jim Morrison or some bohemian character like that. He would turn up to rehearsals drunk, and then just slash his wrists for the attention. Ultimately, Drama Centre was strict, so there was no way it was going to suit him.'

The final year of the course was based around public performances. It was a measure of how much Russell had excelled that he not only survived until the third year, but that he was also given the leading role in the final-year production. He was one of two actors cast as Volpone in Ben Jonson's 1606 satire of the same name.

It was a dream part. It called on Russell to play a sly Italian nobleman who enjoys watching his fortune-hunting friends degrade themselves in a bid to be appointed his heir.

A vicious satire on greed and lust, it is considered one of the best examples of Jacobean comedy.

Not a man to give praise lightly, Christopher Fettes recalls: 'As Russell went into the third year, both his acting teacher Reuven and I had the highest expectations for him. We felt he could be a star. I have no hesitation in saying that he was among two or three of the most gifted people in a very talented group.'

However, as the rehearsals got underway, it quickly became obvious that Russell's drugs and drinking were finally catching up with him. By now, he was out of control, drinking around the clock. Every time Russell was called on to say his speeches, there were embarrassing pauses because he simply didn't know them.

Christopher says: 'Not only did he not come up with any kind of performance, he just hadn't bothered to learn the lines. The result of it was that, despite all the warning and pleading, the fortnight before the play was to be shown, we had to tell him that he would not be able to appear in it. In the end, he just reduced everyone to total despair. I mean, they couldn't rehearse. He didn't seem disturbed or ill or anything like that in rehearsals, although I imagine he had been burning the candle at both ends. It was as if he wished the whole thing would go away. And that is exactly what did happen. It did go away.'

Finally, Christopher was forced to take Russell aside. 'As the director, I had to break the news to him. I told him, "You have got fifteen other people whom you have to consider – and they have got just as many rights as the person playing the leading part." It was as if he knew it was going to happen. He seemed very sad about it. He had no excuses.'

Russell has since told interviewers that he was thrown out with a week to go for 'drug-related behaviour'. But the explanation, according to one contemporary, was simple: the part was huge and Russell just couldn't be bothered to put in the work.

Says Christopher: 'He wasn't expelled. It's just that we couldn't be put in a position like that. We thought he had a brilliant future – but then he fucked it up. So it came as no surprise that when he left the school he did very well. But in a solo capacity.'

Another teacher recalled: 'I don't know anyone who didn't recognize Russell's ability. He had raw, naked, imaginative talent. So it was very upsetting to see him throw it back in the faces of the people who believed in him. Christopher gave him the most wonderful opportunity and Russell wasted it. Everyone was just totally exasperated.'

CHAPTER FOUR

STARTING OUT

'If you are a musician, you are standing on stage going, "Ooh, aren't I sexy?" If you are a comedian, you are going, "Ooh, I'm a bit daft."'

— RUSSELL IN THE *EVENING STANDARD*,
AUGUST 2006

All that was missing was a withering remark from Sharon Osbourne. As Russell Brand stood in the audition room, there was an embarrassing pause before he launched into a pitiful rendition of the Robbie Williams ballad 'Angels'.

Moments before, he had been in the toilet knocking back vodka to calm his nerves. Now, with his shaggy locks glued to his bloated face, Russell was the exact opposite of the clean-cut type the judges were seeking for the line-up of new boy band 5ive.

Grasping a water bottle as a fake microphone, Russell screwed up his eyes in a humiliating attempt to scale the high notes. Even though he'd received passing reviews of his voice at Italia Conti, Russell was the first to admit he was the last person to fit into a manufactured pop band. As Russell later conceded: 'It really was terribly embarrassing. Imagine me with Abs, Doc, Sneazy and the other guys.'

Desperate for stardom, Russell was willing to try anything. He had told his friends back in Grays that he would be famous by the age of twenty. That deadline had now passed. And after mixed feedback from two drama schools, and a growing dependence on drugs and drink, that dream was slipping further away.

In an attempt to find a direction in his life, Russell even consulted a psychic to see if celebrity was anywhere on the distant horizon. Dressed in a fur coat, with no shirt, and swigging once again from a bottle of vodka, Russell arrived for the meeting. The clairvoyant took one look at him – and sagely informed him that his spirit guide was no less than seventies rock singer Marc Bolan.

Funny though it now seems, there was a warning hidden in the quip. Bolan had been a drug user who had died in a car smash at the age of twenty-nine. Most of Russell's friends were starting to wonder if he too would be lucky to see the other side of thirty.

It was clear from his dramatic sacking from *Volpone* that Russell was not temperamentally suited to the demands of fitting into a large cast, with all the preparation and rehearsal that this entailed. Instead, he came to the conclusion that his future lay not in acting, but in stand-up comedy. It suited his quick mind, it gave him a buzz, and improvisation had been the only thing he had been consistently good at both at school and drama college. As a stand-up, the only responsibility was to himself. Rather than saying other people's lines, Russell could come up with his own.

Though he had always been a joker, Russell said that it was only at Drama Centre that he had realized he made people laugh. 'I wanted to be like James Dean, or Marlon Brando, and to have a sort of potency and malevolent, dark sexuality like Jim Morrison. But really I was more like Frank Spencer.'

It had also come to Russell's attention that, for the first time, comedians were being called the new rock stars. Russell was just eighteen when Rob Newman and David Baddiel became the first British comics to fill the 12,000-seat Wembley Arena. Newman's Byronic looks proved it was possible to be funny and a pin-up at the same time. Russell realized he had similar edgy looks, although friends from the period also report that, at times, Russell looked like 'the bastard son of Laurence Llewelyn-Bowen'.

Despite the fact that he had been a promising actor at Drama Centre, he hadn't had a sniff of interest from casting directors, let alone an agent. Yet Russell did not seem to be unduly worried by the fact he had left one more establishment under a cloud of disappointment. 'Russell was a driving force,' recalled a friend. 'He knew he was going to go for stand-up comedy and basically a certificate from a college wasn't going to make any difference.'

By now, Russell had moved out of Willesden Green, where he had been sharing a flat with two mates from drama school, and was living with a loose arrangement of friends in a block of ex-council flats in Bermondsey, south London. Russell had the smallest room because it was the cheapest – although it contained little more than a bundle of clothes and a mattress on the floor. There, he dedicated himself to the task of studying comedy. 'All Russell would watch was comedy videos,' recalled one friend. 'He was totally dedicated to his craft – and wanted to learn from the masters. He studied them to learn about timing, delivery ... every aspect.'

As a child, Russell's biggest heroes had not been sportsmen or singers. They had, with the possible exception of The Smiths' Morrissey, been humorists. It was also a passion he had shared with his dad Ron. In their matey way, they had happily whiled away many hours watching videos of Billy Connolly and Eddie Izzard. The comedians Russell loved most were the ones who spoke honestly about themselves.

But he also adored the quintessential and lugubrious British humorists like Peter Cook and Tony Hancock. *Brass Eye*'s Chris Morris was another inspiration; Russell admired the daring of his spoof current-affairs show, where celebrities and politicians were tricked into supporting absurd political campaigns. The skilful timing and intonation of great British comedies like *Only Fools and Horses* and *Steptoe and Son* also fascinated him.

'I have the rhythm of *Only Fools and Horses* going through my head – those are the riffs that I remember,' he later explained to Bruce Dessau in the *Evening Standard*. 'But if you are a musician, you are standing on stage going, "Ooh, aren't I sexy?" If you are a comedian, you are going, "Ooh, I'm a bit daft." I'm embarrassing, worried and nervous, so comedy is where I belong, it's the only thing that makes me happy.'

His other heroes were the tortured geniuses of American comedy, such as former crack addict Richard Pryor. In the years to come, Russell would be compared to Bill Hicks. In fact, Russell's collection of Hicks's videoed performances was among his most treasured possessions. Hicks had died aged thirty-two, from cancer in 1994. He never worried about offending his audience or cared if they booed him. If they didn't get the joke, that was their problem. Hicks was the first American comic ever to talk freely about masturbation and blow jobs. One of Russell's favourite lines was Hicks's gag: 'Ladies, let me tell you, if men could blow themselves, you would all be here alone tonight. Watching an empty stage.'

Yet Hicks was also filled with righteous indignation. His jokes weren't just meant to be funny – they were meant to kill. Each of his gags, as well as being humorous, made a very serious and direct point. As US chat-show host David Letterman put it, Hicks also had an aura of: '"I'm cocky. Nobody knows me. Too bad." You could almost see him turning his shoulder to the audience.' In Russell's early stand-up, it was a demeanour he would seek to emulate.

Andy Kaufman was yet another blighted comic admired by Russell as a master of absurd. The former *Saturday Night Live* and *Taxi* star had also died young – passing away at thirty-five from lung cancer. With almost all his heroes either dead or addicted to booze or drugs, it was hardly surprising that Russell felt that to be a great comic, it helped to be doomed.

But although Russell loved stand-up, he hated jokes. 'Jokes are an indication your life is not interesting enough,' he later told *Company* magazine. 'I get nervous when people tell me a joke. I keep thinking: "Oh no, where's the bit when I am supposed to laugh?" I'd much rather people were just funny in general.'

Instead, he preferred to pick up erudite references that he could rehash and turn into flights of fancy. He later recalled that he had learned everything he knew about First World War poets Wilfred Owen and Siegfried Sassoon not by reading their verse – but by watching *Blackadder.*

Russell did not yet have the confidence to go it alone. So he hooked up with his closest friend from drama school, Karl Theobald. Their first performance was in a hall behind Drama Centre. From there, they progressed to Hackney Empire Studio, a small venue attached to the main auditorium, where they put on a show absurdly entitled *Theobald and Brand on Ice*.

The flyers for the show pictured Russell with a straight centre parting, the beginnings of a goatee beard and a crazed stare. The show's subject matter was a mixed bag, touching on one of Russell's main preoccupations – warped Victoriana. The piece was one of many to feature his Elephant Man impersonation and explore his fascination with Jack the Ripper.

'The end is nigh,' screamed the show's flyer. 'The Apocalypse approaches. Let's face the Armageddon with a smile. If you'd like to gawp at Elephant Man, Hitler and Christ and discover what finally made Jack the Ripper crack, then, as Elvis Presley said, "You've come to the right place."'

While he liked to play it for laughs, the angry young man in Russell wanted to change the world – but didn't know how. At heart, he was an anarchist who never voted in his life. His politics were loosely based on his working-class roots and his fascination with revolution.

Russell loved comedy terrorism – and anything that shocked and upset the status quo. He hooked up with a left-wing writer and film-maker by the name of John Rogers. One memorable afternoon, Russell put on his Elephant Man act to approach passers-by for John's documentary about the degeneration of Spitalfields Market. Not surprisingly, following complaints from rattled members of the public, the police moved him along.

Russell also appeared in John's brainchild, *The Soapbox Cabaret*, a political revue which played at the fringes of the Labour party conferences in Bournemouth and Brighton in 1999 and 2000.

'It was about poking fun at Labour – and cabinet ministers,' recalled a former member of the cast. 'It was a way to make it simple for audiences to understand just what was going on, so they weren't having the wool pulled over their eyes.'

Despite the serious message, they were not always the most polished performances. 'At one point, the stage caught fire, but we just carried on singing and dancing through it. Sometimes, we would go on stage drunk, literally, and it would be a mess. Other times, it would be amazing and we would do encores.'

With costumes including fishnets, feather boas and sequined vests, the cabaret was a cross between a music-hall drag show and a fringe meeting. Russell and the rest of the crew dressed variously as Tony Blair, Alastair Campbell and Bill Clinton. Russell was apt to burst into improvised show tunes anyway, so he was in his element singing numbers like 'Are You On Message?', 'Welcome To The New World Order (Don't Let Bill Near Your Daughter)', and 'Low-Fat New Labour Dinner – Terence Conran Says It's A Vote-Winner'.

It was probably the first and last time Russell never got a

namecheck. But the review in communist daily paper the *Morning Star* was rapturous. It called *The Soapbox Cabaret* 'subversive' and 'a reaction against the narrow confines of debate, which have been made even more narrow by the Millbank mob'. The review rhapsodized: 'It creates an arena, where all debate is possible and ideas such as the Third Way and ethical foreign policy can be given the thorough lampooning they deserve – with a high kick and a song.'

The show at the Bournemouth Roundhouse Hotel was named Best Party of the 1999 Labour Conference by *The Independent* – and the cabaret returned to Brighton the following year.

Otherwise, work was thin on the ground – and Russell was scratching to make a living. On paper, he hardly qualified for anything except bar work. But he had heard about a language school where they would train you in just five days – so Russell applied to work at the Callan School in Oxford Street, central London. Luckily for him, the teaching method was a quick-fire technique where he could use his dramatic talents. Teachers were supposed to use mime and movement to help students understand what was going on. The aim was to make classes 'dynamic and energetic'.

Russell stood on a podium and quizzed students at high speed from a textbook. The idea was to get them to break the habit of mentally translating English into their mother tongue before answering. To start with, Russell was an enthusiastic teacher. Soon, however, it was observed that his class was not making much progress – mainly because Russell had started bunking off to smoke dope in nearby Soho Square.

When Russell asked for two weeks' holiday to Spain, his request was refused on the grounds that he had to stay and help his pupils catch up. Russell went anyway. On his return, the principal demanded to know where he'd been. 'I said: "I have got some terrible news,"' he remembered later. '"I had to have two weeks off because I've got Aids." No one believed me. But it was such a terrible lie that people couldn't question it.'

At the end of each day, the students would meet in the pub. Russell had already noticed a lively Spanish girl by the name of Amanda, who had a curvaceous full figure and straight dark hair. She worked as a bar manager in Ibiza. When the clubbing season was over, she would come to London to try to get her English up to scratch. It was to be the start of Russell's most important romantic relationship.

'Russell was totally besotted with Amanda, head over heels in love,' recalls a friend. 'It was the first time he was really serious about a woman. She wasn't necessarily what you would expect from Russell's girlfriend. She was a lovely girl, quite down-to-earth and homely. She had dark hair, big lips and very expressive eyes – she was charming to look at – and very friendly and funny with it.'

Yet Amanda was more than a match for him: quite eccentric in her own way – and with a strong personality. When Russell was with her, he was like 'a little pussy cat'. He was always on his best behaviour.

Even the serious language barrier wasn't enough to come between them. 'She didn't speak very good English and he didn't speak very good Spanish – although he did buy some language tapes. But they had something more powerful than that. There was a serious willingness on Russell's part to make their relationship work – at first, anyway.'

Within months, Russell astonished his friends by talking about marriage – he was full of romantic enthusiasm about his new affair. Despite the fact he was only twenty-five, most pals were surprised but relieved, believing that Amanda could bring him the security he needed.

Although Russell's love life was experiencing a period of stability, ultimately the year was to end on a sad note. Just before Christmas – on 21 December 1999 – his nan Jen died at Romford's Old Church Hospital. She had just turned eighty-nine. Jen's health had been deteriorating for some time; and she had been suffering from forgetfulness, something that broke Russell's heart to see. Eventually, she died of pneumonia.

At the funeral, Russell cut a heartbreakingly dignified figure. 'I don't think I have ever seen Russell look as handsome as he did that day. It was the first time I had seen Russell suited and booted. He looked immaculate,' recalls one of the mourners. 'He was devastated by it. Jen would have done anything for him. He was her refuge from everything. Even now, he still misses her.' For the service, Russell wrote a poem describing how his grandmother had gone to a better place. It described the meals she had cooked him and the pet names they had for one another. 'The church was packed, but there wasn't a dry eye in the house when he read it out.'

After Christmas, Russell returned for a new term at the language school. His timetable meant that he could pursue his comedy at the same time – and increasingly Russell was finding the confidence to perform as a lone stand-up. He loved the freedom and found the complete lack of censorship liberating.

As Russell later told the *Birmingham Post*: 'You don't need anyone to give you a job in stand-up. You can just do it above a pub, or by a pub, or near a pub, or under a pub. As long as there is a pub somewhere in the proximity, stand-up comedy can work. I was good at it, so it was easy to get a foothold.'

Gradually, he started to venture out on his own, although in those days, Russell was not so much funny as outrageous. A friend who saw Russell's first solo gig said: 'It was a state. Russell was messing around with drugs, but it was not yet serious. He was really jumping around a lot between things, trying to decide what to do.'

His dad Ron recalled driving Russell to an early performance in Kent. The pub was crammed. Ron sat in the audience reading a newspaper, waiting for his son to come on stage – but all the time anxiously fearing that Russell wouldn't go through with it.

When his mobile rang, he was convinced it was Russell ready to make his excuses and leave. But he was wrong. Russell had never been so sure of anything in his life. He took to the stage and got a great reception. Ron recalled: 'He did the show. It was brilliant and everyone loved him. It was one of my proudest moments.'

CHAPTER FIVE

ON THE COMEDY MAP

'While each of the three newcomers acquitted themselves admirably, it is Brand who has "Star of the Future" tattooed beneath his Calvin Kleins.'

— JANE-ANN PURDY IN *THE SCOTSMAN*,
AUGUST 2000

By the year 2000, when he turned twenty-five, Russell had performed no more than five solo stand-up gigs. But that didn't stop him entering one of the toughest talent shows in the business. The Hackney Empire New Act of the Year contest was a prestigious showcase for up-and-coming comedians. It was, as Russell later recalled, 'the most significant gig' of his life.

After a gruelling round of heats, Russell had made it to the final thirteen. Now, in the Victorian grandeur of one of London's most historic venues, he had just eight minutes to make an impression on the panel of judges, which was comprised of comedy critics and professionals.

Russell had everything to play for. The previous entrants were like a Who's Who of British comedy from the last decade. They included Rob Newman, Harry Hill, David Baddiel and Ardal O'Hanlon. Russell's imagination was also captured by the Hackney Empire's history. Built in 1901 in the heyday of the music hall, the theatre's stage had once been graced by Marie Lloyd, Charlie Chaplin and Stan Laurel. Now Russell was to join that star-studded list.

That year, the competition was a mixed bag, and Russell felt he was in with a good chance. His rivals included a Sikh comedian whose main gag was a flashing turban, a pair of nameless mime artists and a cerebral-palsy sufferer taking an irreverent look at life with disabilities.

Fortified as ever by some last-minute swigs of vodka,

Russell was third up on the bill. When the red light came on and he stepped on to the stage, he later recalled that it felt as if he had stepped into the middle of a huge crimson wedding cake.

What followed next could best be described as comedy anarchy. Aggressive and confrontational, Russell filled the stage like a whirlwind. It was a political tirade, which ranged from his upbringing in Grays to Care in the Community in Hackney. As ever, he relied on the adrenalin to get him through. As he later recalled in the *Sunday Herald*: 'There was a moment when my mind went empty and I thought: "Oh no, I'm in front of all these people and I've got nothing to say," and then, there are like tendrils of inspiration you can grab and it's all right again.'

The eventual winner, Paul Hickman, recalled that the tone of Russell's performance was very much: 'If you don't like it, then you can fuck off.' 'The act was much odder than it is now. Amongst the audience, the reaction was a mixture of confusion and laughter. Russell had a strange way about him in those days. He was still working on that sort of eloquent cockney, lower-middle-class foppery.'

When Russell's eight minutes were up, there was a polite smattering of applause. While no one could claim Russell was hysterically funny, there was something about him – his passion, confidence and good looks – that nevertheless left an impression. At the time, the prevailing trend in comedy was for blokey, *Loaded*-style comedians. Russell was different. 'He stood out as not your average, matey, man-on-the-street stand-up,' recalled one transfixed member of the audience. 'He was young and lanky. He had longish hair and a dandyish air. He exuded a slightly manic nervous energy. He was accomplished, but there was something a tiny bit vain and annoying about him.'

Even the judges and critics who hated his performance

found him impossible to ignore. Writing in *The Times* in March 2000, judge Clive Davis called Russell's act 'a mad urban rant', which reminded him of 'Ben Elton without the jokes. Ben Elton with jokes is irritating enough, thank you.' Meanwhile, critic Derek Smith in *The Stage* also found Russell a little bit too full-on – but still saw some potential. 'Russell Brand was in your face, strutting the stage and venting his spleen about politics, world hunger and a loony in his local park: his full-volume, agitated tirade became a bit overpowering after a while. If Brand calmed down and varied the pace of his puns, he would be far more effective. He has some good earthy material, which got a good audience reaction and bodes well for the future.'

When the winners were announced, Russell had come joint fourth in the line-up. He was not too disappointed, though – his idol Eddie Izzard had made only third place. And even if he had not walked off with the first prize, he had caught the eye of a couple of important players in the comedy industry.

Known as Scotland's Queen of Comedy, Karen Koren was artistic director of the Gilded Balloon, a key comedy venue at the Edinburgh Festival. In her time, the straight-talking comedy boss had helped launch the careers of Steve Coogan and Phil Kay. The moment she set eyes on Russell, she knew he had something special. She recalled: 'None of the other judges rated him, but I liked him from the start. Russell was an angry young man. He wanted to change the world. But he had a real intelligence about him.'

Nigel Klarfeld – boss of a comedy management agency, Bound and Gagged – had also spotted a spark in Russell. 'He hadn't gone down particularly well with the audience, but as a manager, you don't necessarily look at what the audience want. You look at his potential for the future. The eventual winner, Paul Hickman, stormed the gig. But even though he came virtually nowhere in the competition, Russell had something about him. He hadn't done that many gigs at that point. He was as new as you can get – and his act came across as very anarchic. But of the line-up, he was the only one who had some "wow factor" about him.'

Before taking him on, though, Nigel decided to see Russell perform one more time to make sure. A few weeks later, in April, he went to see him perform at Downstairs at the King's Head in Crouch End, north London. It confirmed what he had seen at the Hackney Empire. 'Russell just looked great. He was very good-looking and cool. He had long hair and sideburns, and was just dressed in jeans and a vest – but he looked edgy. I saw him as having pop-star potential. He was also highly intelligent and he had charisma – and you can't invent that.'

Though the raw materials were there, there was still work to be done. 'I told him he needed to make himself more accessible. I felt that if Russell could merge his comedy better with how he looked, he had great potential.' Nigel's suggestion was that Russell try television presenting – and in particular MTV.

Meanwhile, encouraged by Karen, Russell took her up on her suggestion of coming to the Gilded Balloon to perform at the Edinburgh Fringe Festival in August of that year. With some financial help from his dad, he booked a room. When it became clear that he didn't have enough material to do the whole show on his own, he invited fellow Hackney competitors Mark Felgate and Shappi Khorsandi to join him for a three-hander, mysteriously entitled *Pablo Diablo's Cryptic Triptych*.

As a complete unknown in a town packed with new acts, it was essential that Russell did everything he could to advertise the show. But he hated handing out flyers. When he met some delinquents in the street from a council estate in Leith, he paid them to do it for him. 'I found these little kids, aged between eight and twelve, who lived on an estate round the corner,' Russell later recalled in an interview with the *Daily Record*.

'They were on the street one day, being really naughty, lighting matches and throwing things about. I really loved them, but they kept getting into trouble. They came into the Gilded Balloon production offices and stole condoms off the desk.

'Eventually, they ended up in my show. I was like, "I love kids, me. And kids love me too." Then I'd put my arms around them and give them a cuddle. They'd hug me and be all smiling and stuff. Then they'd stick a sign on my back saying "wanker" or something.'

Venue director Karen Koren remembers that Russell wasn't always funny, but he was usually outrageous. 'Russell was only hilarious because he used to get all the kids around him like flies. They were real tearaway urchins and Russell was like a young Fagin. He had them just where he wanted them. I adored Russell, but I had to treat him like a naughty schoolboy. I gave him rows all the time. I was telling him: "For heaven's sake, you can't have kids in the show. You know it's against the law!"'

In the end, because he was in contravention of child labour legislation – and also because his primary-school sidekicks were spitting at the punters – Karen wrote Russell an official letter of complaint.

'I had to sack the children, which was pretty embarrassing,' he said later. 'I was like, "Sorry, kids, bad news. Want a cigarette?" They were like: "If you sack us, we'll huvtae go back tae stealing." I told them: "You are breaking my heart here, but I need to let you go."'

Despite his confident appearance, before each show, Russell would need to disappear for a while to collect his thoughts. 'He would hide himself away in the toilet to psyche himself up,' recalled a friend. 'He needed to lose the fear first.'

Russell's nerves meant that he found it easiest to relax into his performance if he made his entrance as his favourite character, the Elephant Man. Limping towards the mike, he delivered his material in wheezing John Merrick tones. The slightly sinister opening set the scene for a show that explored the darker side of human existence, touching on everything from suicide to child abuse. In a sign of things to come, Russell also turned to the tabloids for inspiration, deconstructing the hysterical tone of the *News of the World*'s campaign against paedophiles. Full of dramatic gestures, and veering between the cockney loudmouth at one extreme and erudite actor at the other, it was a mesmerizing performance.

Yet every night, Russell's act was slightly different. Unlike other novice comics who stuck to their routines, Russell improvised. 'He took the piss out of people who just repeated the same thing word for word every night,' recalled a friend, who visited him at the Fringe. 'He prided himself on the fact he never did the same gig twice.'

He was only starting out. But already Russell knew how to play the publicity game. Throughout his career, he was to have an unerring ability to charm the people that mattered, whether they were journalists or important industry contacts. Amid hot competition, Russell managed to persuade every leading newspaper from *The Scotsman* to *The Stage* to see his show. When Karen herself singled him out for mention in an interview with the *Glasgow Herald* as 'a very funny guy', it was as good as his anointment as the next big thing in comedy.

Female reviewers, in particular, were taken by Russell's good looks. One woman critic said he strode across the stage like 'a Spanish pin-up' and described him as 'tall and swoonsome'. Jane-Ann Purdy in *The Scotsman* was equally enamoured: 'Tossing his long locks, he cuts loose and enjoyed an audience who were soon hanging on his every word.' Out of the three performers in the show, she predicted it was Russell who had 'star of the future' tattooed beneath his Calvin Kleins.

Male reviewers were also impressed by his magnetism.

David Belcher of the *Glasgow Herald* raved: 'Russell Brand looks like a male model, or the great-great-great-grandson of romantic seducer Heathcliff. Russell's got loads of brains and lots of education, all of which he puts to good use in ruminating wordily about a wide range of singular preoccupations. Oh, yeah – and Russell's pretty jolly funny, and he'll be funnier still when he's developed more stagecraft and stopped being quite so eager to please.'

A slightly more sanguine Steve Ben, of comedy website Chortle, called Russell's material 'patchy, with oversimplified political stuff sitting alongside distinctly funnier general observations. However, bounding with enthusiasm and confidence, Brand is eminently watchable and, with a bit more polish, will surely be a success.'

Russell was on the comedy map. Not wanting to waste a moment, he had also got to the final nine out of 500 entrants in regional heats of another key talent show, *So You Think You're Funny?*, hosted by Graham Norton at the Gilded Balloon. He lost out to a call-centre worker from Melbourne called Drew Rokos.

The 2000 festival was notable for one other important reason. While he was in Edinburgh, Russell had auditioned for a play, one of two pieces that year written by an up-and-coming humorist and playwright by the name of Trevor Lock.

Well educated, with a degree in philosophy from University College London, Trevor had also played cricket for his home county of Northamptonshire. Since giving up his dreams of playing professionally, he had enjoyed a flourishing TV career, thanks to performances on Lee and Herring's *This Morning with Richard Not Judy*. Two years older than Russell, he was an old hand at the Fringe, having performed there since 1996.

As an established talent, Trevor could easily have been dismissive of the budding star. To Russell, he seemed a mysterious figure: 'He was this person you never used to know anything about, you never used to know quite what was going on with Trevor Lock because he never used to tell you anything. But he was lovely to me and the play was dead good.'

The show was entitled *There's Something You Should Know*. Trevor played the part of Terry Franklin, who is killed in a car crash. Unable to accept his sudden death, he decides to carry on as normal. He is allowed one last chance to stay on earth to complete some unfinished business – a love affair with his childhood sweetheart, June. Russell played his laddish flatmate Pete, who helps Terry declare his hidden love.

The production received good reviews – and the chemistry between Trevor and Russell got a special mention in *The Scotsman*, which applauded 'the scenes with Lock and his laddish sidekick [Russell], where he philosophizes on life, love and the opposite sex'. Russell also appeared in Trevor's other piece, which was about a man who lives alone and thinks his furniture is talking to him. Russell played his cynical American TV set.

Apart from their performances, Russell and Trevor did not spend much time together during the Festival. But they found they shared the same absurd sense of humour and a rare ability to turn big ideas into accessible comedy. Although in years to come the balance of power was to change, it was to be the start of a fruitful relationship; with Trevor eventually becoming one of Russell's closest collaborators.

Russell returned to London proud of what he had achieved. Already he was being spoken of as a star in waiting. In his Chortle website profile, he was described as 'a lively, fast-talking newcomer who dashes about the stage like a hurricane. This impressive bombastic delivery unfortunately covers some weakish material, although there are signs this is improving. One to watch for sheer stage presence alone.'

To capitalize on his success, Russell was determined to

clock up as many gigs as he could. His manager Nigel booked him on a package show of comedians touring universities.

As Russell performed more, Nigel was encouraged by his drive to succeed – and also by the improvement in his stand-up routines. However, he was concerned that Russell's performances could be inconsistent. 'Russell was definitely a man on a mission. You could feel that he wanted to get there. He talked about wanting to go all the way. I don't think even he knew how he was going to do it. He just wanted to be successful. He was confident moving about the stage. He had no fear in him. If audiences didn't like him, he didn't seem overly bothered by the bad reaction. He turned up to all the gigs, although at times his performance was quite erratic. Occasionally, there were complaints about his manner. Promoters sometimes found him over the top and too anarchic.'

It was only later, says Nigel, that he realized the cause. 'Russell never did drugs in front of me, although he used to drink quite a lot. I never had a clue about the severity of the drugs at the time. However, what I have read subsequently explains a lot.'

As Russell continued to drink heavily, he never took the time to write any new material. The result was that he would go on stage – and have to think of something there and then. Most of the time, he was relying on shock rather than humour. Dead animals were among his favourite props. At one memorable performance at 92 East in Brick Lane, he performed a whole nativity play with a cast of dead mice.

As one fellow comic, who was also on the stand-up scene at the time, recalled: 'You would never use the word "funny" to describe Russell. He was more of a spectacle. He never wrote jokes in a structured way. It was a performance – mesmerizing and exciting. I think when you were as pained and tortured as he was, the last thing you wanted to do was be funny.'

Hyped up and desperate for success, Russell was so full-on

that he could sometimes come over as a bit strange. His intensity could be off-putting, and many people who met him for the first time hated him on sight. However, his closest friends felt that Russell's aggressively extrovert persona was a mask he put on to keep the world out.

As one intimate recalled: 'Russell was a bit of a Jekyll and Hyde. He had an insecure side. There were many times when he felt lacking in confidence and he wanted a heart-to-heart for reassurance. When he was acting on stage, he would turn into a different person. The face he showed to the world was "the performance Russell", because it was easier to show a mask to the world than his real self. He found it easier to face the crowd when he was not showing them who he really was. It meant that he was most comfortable surrounded by a small circle of friends whom he knew and trusted, and luckily at the time he had a really good bunch of people around him. When he was with them, there were many times when he was quiet and thoughtful.'

Russell's moodiness was also a symptom of his suspected bipolar disorder. There were times when he would sit for hours in silence watching reruns of comedy classics. Far from being the life and soul of the party at social gatherings, he would often do nothing but retreat into a corner and look furtively around the room.

Another friend agreed: 'I have always felt Russell is a little bit shy. There are two Russells. There's the explosion you see and there's the real guy who, when you get him on a serious subject, is quite sensitive and well read. When you actually got talking to him in quiet moments, you realized he wasn't the cockney loudmouth, but someone who was very intelligent. Initially, he was so in your face that he could come across as a bit mad and annoying. But when you really got to know him, he had an innocence and sweetness about him that it was hard not to like.'

The year was to end on a high note when Russell landed a part in a glossy cinema commercial for Danish chewing gum Stimorol Big Fresh. The ad was shown only in northern Europe. For budget reasons, it was being shot in Cuba.

Russell couldn't believe his luck. He was to spend a fortnight in a luxury villa, complete with swimming pool, in Havana, with three other young comedians he already knew from the circuit. What's more, they only had to work every two days. The rest of the time they had to themselves to explore the island.

The ad's director, Søren Bonnelle, remembered he picked Russell from a line-up at a casting in London. 'I liked Russell's attitude. He was good-looking without being too "modelly". He just made everything around him funny.'

It was an off-the-wall commercial. At a party, Russell asks why his geeky friend is wearing a vet's collar. He replies that it is to disguise his bad breath. With his curly hair in a mullet style down to his shoulders, and wearing a red vest, Russell looks like a young Kevin Keegan.

En route to Cuba, Russell set the tone for the whole trip when he wandered off at the airport – and came back with three adoring girls in tow.

'To be honest, Russell came across as a bit weird at that point,' recalled one of the party. 'We were all show-offs, but Russell was the level above, really. It took a few days before you could work out if you liked him or not. But when you did, he was just great. He was an adventurer. With anyone else, you would have ended up at all the obvious tourist spots. With Russell, you would find him leading you into some ghetto – usually because he was trying to score some drugs. We had a great time.'

For a young man who loved nothing better than to sleep with prostitutes, Cuba was a dream destination. The moment the boys walked into a nightclub, they would find themselves inundated with attractive women offering them sex. It did not take long to exhaust Russell's budget. When he took two prostitutes back to his room one night, he discovered that he didn't have the money to pay them both.

At 4 a.m., his housemates were woken by the sound of Russell banging on their doors, begging to borrow $200. Later that morning, the hookers had taken up position on the sofa – and despite some polite small talk, it was clear they were not going anywhere without the cash. However, if there had been threats exchanged during the night, by now the negotiations seemed quite civilized. In desperation, Russell rang home to get some money wired to his account, so he could finally get them to go away. When they did, it was discovered they had cleaned the house out of every last toiletry product, from the toothpaste to the antiperspirant.

'Russell hadn't seemed particularly panicky,' recalled one of the group. 'He was just trying to do the right thing and find the rest of the money. Although there was a lot of fuss about it afterwards – there were complaints from the villa's owners to the production crew – Russell was pretty blasé about it. It was just all a bit of an adventure, being a lad in your mid-twenties in Cuba and being paid stupid money.

'Russell has always said his life is a string of embarrassing incidents strung together by him talking about the embarrassing incidents – and that was certainly one of them.'

As a young teenager, Russell (middle row, second left) considered himself chubby. Here he is pictured at the height of his bulimia in class 4KY, age fourteen, in his school picture at Grays School, Essex.

you might boo es femous es me one day if so see you at the top bum biggest LOVE

er

IN PORTRAITURE

R
y
s
s
V

B
r
A
N
o

The first glimpse of Russell in *Bugsy Malone*, the production which changed the course of his life. His co-star was girlfriend Melanie Gillingham (pictured far left), to whom he inscribed this message when they left school (*above right*).

Opposite: Mean and moody: Russell, age sixteen, in a publicity shot sent to his first drama school, the Italia Conti Academy.

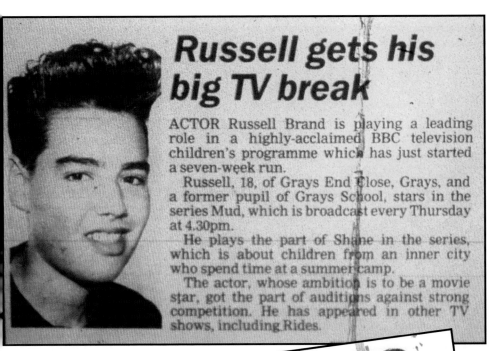

Russell gets his big TV break

ACTOR Russell Brand is playing a leading role in a highly-acclaimed BBC television children's programme which has just started a seven-week run.

Russell, 18, of Grays End Close, Grays, and a former pupil of Grays School, stars in the series Mud, which is broadcast every Thursday at 4.30pm.

He plays the part of Shane in the series, which is about children from an inner city who spend time at a summer camp.

The actor, whose ambition is to be a movie star, got the part of auditions against strong competition. He has appeared in other TV shows, including Rides.

This week Essex, tomorrow the world: Russell shows an early talent for self-publicity with this piece in his local paper, the *Thurrock Gazette*, in which he modestly states that his ambition is to be a 'movie star'.

Right: Russell's first job out of drama school was playing kids' counsellor Shane in BBC children's show *Mud*.

Russell gave a convincing performance as tearaway Billy Case in an episode of *The Bill* broadcast in October 1994. Here he is pictured with DS Chris Deakin, played by Shaun Scott.

Billy's police interview. One of his most memorable lines was: 'I never did any of that!'

The imposing façade of the Drama Centre in Chalk Farm, north London. When Russell's part in *The Bill* failed to lead to other roles, he decided he needed more training.

Bad hair day: Russell sports an extraordinary Kevin Keegan-style mullet in a commercial for chewing gum Stimorol Big Fresh in 2000. The ad was shot in Cuba, where Russell took the opportunity to live it up during filming.

October 2001: Russell hosts the *Muzik* Magazine Dance Awards.

With co-host June Sarpong.

One of Russell's first jobs for MTV was touring Britain to promote new US stunt show *Jackass*.

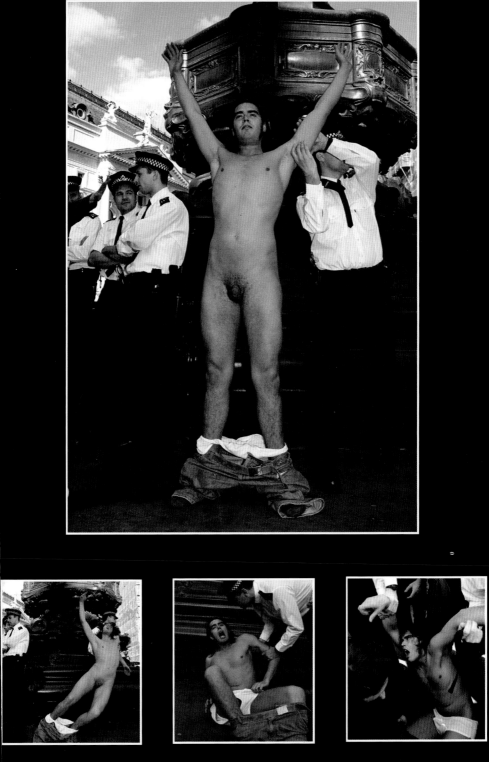

'I am Television!': In a bid to create 'a happening' for his new documentary series, Russell stripped in front of the statue Eros in Piccadilly Circus during the 2002 May Day riots. As the police dragged him away, Russell feigned an epileptic fit.

A pensive moment during the shooting of 'My Old Tart' for the *Re:Brand* documentary series in Eastbourne in 2002.

Veteran actress Wendy Danvers agreed to be swept off to Eastbourne for a 'dirty weekend' with Russell.

CHAPTER SIX

LIVING IT UP

'I thought, "I could spend all this money on heroin, that'll cheer me up."'

— RUSSELL IN THE *BIRMINGHAM POST*, REMEMBERING 2001

Russell had just taken a break in the filming for his new MTV show when he saw a group of people huddled round a television screen laughing. Curious, he went over to see what the fuss was about. As he drew near, he was both stunned and elated to find that the cause of the hilarity was some of the off-the-cuff one-liners he had just filmed for *Dance Floor Chart*.

For Russell, it was the most exciting moment of his career so far. Just a couple of months ago, he had been a starving language-school teacher, moonlighting as a stand-up comedian. Now, at the age of twenty-five, he had a promising career in television; the charisma he had on stage was making an easy transition to the small screen.

Russell had first come to the attention of MTV talent spotters when they had seen his show at the Edinburgh Festival the summer before, in August 2000. If they were impressed then, Russell's showreel confirmed it for them. With the help of Mark Pinheiro – his flatmate who worked at the TV station – he had submitted a short, edited collection of his best work. Frank, confessional and brimming with energy and wit, the first twenty seconds were enough to hook them.

From early 2001, Russell was to host *Dance Floor Chart* – a weekly show based around the hottest clubbing hits of the moment. So that he could focus on his new job, Russell moved out of his communal flat in an ex-council property in

Bermondsey and into a stunning loft-style conversion in Yorkton Street, Hackney.

Dance Floor Chart could have been made for Russell. Initially, the idea was for Russell to do straightforward links between the records – or to get the clubbers themselves to introduce the next track. Instead, the show quickly turned into a platform for Russell's off-the-wall comedy ideas. As he toured the country's nightclubs, he took absurdity to new heights. He often screwed the script up into a ball, chucked it in the bin and let his imagination run wild. Some of his classic lines included: 'I went to the garden centre the other day. But I found that the garden centre wasn't in the centre of my garden at all. Have I been ripped off?' To another girl, he posed the question: 'Do you find me more or less attractive than an angry wasp?' Utterly bemused, most of his interviewees just responded with 'You what?' or 'Mental!'

To begin with, at least, MTV bosses were thrilled with Russell. His ad-libbed humour and edgy rock-star looks meant they couldn't stop boasting about their 'brilliant' new signing. They showered him with more work, and offered him slots presenting the live afternoon kids' show, *Select*.

When they also needed a presenter to go on a ten-day promotional tour for new US stunt show *Jackass*, Russell was the obvious choice. Otherwise known as the 'Egg on your Face and your Shoes' tour, it involved young men discovering how many eggs they could swallow in one go before they vomited. The highlight was the Belfast leg of the tour, where one contestant managed to down twenty-eight. While it wasn't exactly BAFTA-winning material, Russell thought it was hilarious. 'It all adds to the fun,' he said at the time. 'I know some people will find it disgusting, but to me it's pretty funny.'

Moreover, however hard the contestants might have tried, they had a tough job beating Russell for behaving badly.

Indeed, from the moment he stepped inside MTV's Camden Lock studios, it was as if he felt it was part of his job description. In Russell's mind, notoriety was the quickest route to fame.

Russell's glamorous new job also meant looking the part, and he was determined to perfect his image as a louche rock star. However, it was not as effortless as it seemed. Russell's wardrobe had always had a dandyish dramatic edge and he liked to wear his clothes as tight as possible. Neighbours of his gran in Dagenham recalled he had once looked like an escaped cult member, when he went through a phase of wearing all white with open-toe sandals.

Now that he was at MTV, he had his own stylist. When Sharon Smith first laid eyes on Russell, she was appalled. He was wearing a cropped T-shirt with his belly showing. 'I thought: "We've got a lot of work to do here,"' she told *Glamour* magazine. 'From the beginning, he was an exhibitionist.' Sharon was a salt-of-the-earth type from a council estate in Rotherhithe, south London. She and Russell instantly hit it off and she became a close friend. Four years later, she was to play a key role in reinventing Russell as a gothic Lothario. For now, she set about sharpening up his image, and calling in expensive designer clothes for him to try. Russell took his grooming so seriously he even hired a maid to come in just to iron his flash new wardrobe.

Russell's crowning glory had always been his hair. Generally, he preferred it long. Later, when he grew bored of his curls, he would have a go at straightening them with tongs. The look was completed with twice-weekly visits to the Electric Beach tanning salon. With his sideburns down to his jawline, he looked like a better-looking version of Gaz Coombes from Supergrass.

Then, of course, there was the money. For the first time in his life, Russell had cash in his pocket. His basic wage for *Dance*

Floor Chart was around £500 a week – a small fortune for a young man who sometimes hadn't had the change for a loaf of bread. As MTV deluged him with work, the cash rolled in.

When he started at the station, Russell was drinking heavily and smoking weed. He usually had some gin or vodka concealed about his person. A cloud of marijuana smoke also seemed to follow him wherever he went. As his friend and MTV colleague Matt Morgan later recalled, Russell had 'a little pipe with skunk in it almost always attached to his face'.

Now Russell could afford Class A narcotics as well. Crack made Russell behave in a silly way. He had always gloried in the absurd, but crack meant he thought nothing of carrying a pig around in a blanket and pretending it was a baby. On another occasion, he ran out of the MTV studio and jumped on the roof of a Maserati sports car belonging to one of the senior directors.

Heroin, on the other hand, sedated him. Russell had smoked it only a couple of times since the day, five years earlier, when some Turkish teenagers had offered it to him at a discount rate outside Hackney Central station. At £40 a hit, he could now afford it every day if he wanted it.

Drugs were also Russell's way of fending off depression and tedium. 'I thought, "I could spend all this money on heroin, that'll cheer me up." I was trying to fill a void. I've got a lot of energy and a high capacity for consuming experience. I need stimulus and something happening or I get bored.'

Wherever he went on his tour of the country's nightclubs for *Dance Floor Chart*, he left a trail of destruction. Rashers of bacon were left behind pictures, and a pig's head Russell had been using as a puppet in a comedy sketch got dumped in a hotel bath. As well as the cost of putting everything right, Russell ran up large room-service bills for an assortment of items, from designer swimming trunks to lettuce leaves for his pet snails.

Within three months of his arrival at MTV, word of his antics was already reaching the press. In March, staff at the Leeds Hilton found a shoebox containing two African snails. After buying the creatures from a stall at Brixton Market, Russell had taken them around Britain for the *Jackass* tour. Hotel staff promptly handed them over to RSPCA inspectors.

Seizing his moment in the limelight, Russell played the incident for all it was worth, and issued an emotional appeal for his pets' return, insisting he was 'a responsible snail-bearer'. His plea was somewhat undermined by the fact that in one interview Russell named them as Foxy and Handsome, and in another as Bertie and Wilbur. 'I miss them and want them back, poor little fellas,' he said. 'The minute I realized they were gone, I was devastated. I grew kind of close to them – well, as close as any man can get to a mollusc.' The charity, however, took a firm line and refused to hand them back, saying: 'These are exotic species that require specialist care and to take them to a hotel and leave them there is, at best, irresponsible.'

Among the perks of his job was Russell's account with taxi firm Addison Lee – or 'Addison Free' as he referred to it. Using it like a personal chauffeur service, he had cabs at his beck and call to take him to his drug dealer in east London, or even to pick up his mum Babs from Grays for a day trip to London and back home again, a 40-mile round trip. He booked one of their cars to transport him and his mate Matt on a sailing holiday on the Norfolk Broads. When a friend of a friend visited from Europe, he got a free guided tour of the sights from the back of one of the firm's black people carriers.

One of Russell's favourite diversions was lap-dancing clubs, and he was soon a regular at establishments like Spearmint Rhino. To ensure a VIP welcome and the best table, he would ring ahead, putting on a heavy Scottish accent and pretending to be his own agent, calling himself silly names like Jock McGee or Jack Starburst. On more than one occasion, he was thrown out for drunken conduct.

There was no Jock, or Jack, for that matter. The reality was that Russell had parted company with his manager Nigel soon after he arrived at MTV. He moved to KBJ, an agency which specialized in representing TV presenters. It had been set up two years earlier by former newsreader Joanna Kaye, and already had some big names on its books, including Dermot Murnaghan and Kirsty Young.

Russell's presenting style couldn't have been more different. On *Dance Floor Chart*, he came across as a maniac unleashed with a microphone, blurting out whatever came into his head, whenever he felt like saying it. At any opportunity, he would also launch into ad-hoc show tunes on any subject from the virtues of polystyrene plates to the state of the weather. On one occasion, he wandered around a festival site, shouting: 'Whose are these ball bags?' – an early outing of one of his favourite catchphrases.

Off screen, too, Russell was prone to outlandish and, at times, prima donna-ish behaviour. When his usual Mercedes car didn't come to pick him up, he refused to get into the alternative vehicle. Some of his colleagues found him difficult to get to know and Russell felt there were few people he got on with. Nevertheless, there was one notable exception.

Matt Morgan was working as an intern at MTV to get some experience in television. He was a bright boy, also from a working-class background, who had left Dartford Grammar School in Kent with A levels in English Literature, Psychology, Sociology and Art. Like most people, Matt had heard about Russell long before he met him. In the interview for his position, he had been told about the station's 'brilliantly funny' new presenter. Matt, however, hated Russell on sight, dismissing him as a perma-tanned loud-mouthed pretty boy.

Fortuitously, the pair were thrown together when Matt was sent over to Dublin to help film *Dance Floor Chart*. As 'the talent', Russell was supposed to be up in business class. But a booking mistake meant he got stuck back in economy next to Matt. During the journey, the two of them got chatting and discovered a shared love for many of the same comedians. Like Russell, Matt loved Peter Cook and Tony Hancock, and even understood Russell's obsession with the Elephant Man.

That night, the new pals had dinner together. Matt, who had a bear-like masculine presence about him, balked when Russell turned up in a vest and tiny pair of shorts. To his deep shame, Matt realized that everyone in the restaurant thought they were a gay couple. As Russell later recalled: 'He was my muse back then, that boy; I looked over at him and I knew everything would be all right. And we've stayed friends ever since that beautiful day.'

In Matt, Russell found a soulmate with a similar background and the intelligence to keep up with his absurd tangents. Matt was two years younger than Russell, but mature for his age. Although he enjoyed a drink, he was not into drugs. When Russell's ideas became too outlandish, Matt brought him back down to earth again. And if Russell started taking himself too seriously, Matt was on hand to remind him not to be so ridiculous. If Russell ever ran out of inspiration for his mad one-liners on *Dance Floor Chart*, Matt fed him a few ideas – and then Russell would be off again. Before long, he was promoted to Russell's assistant. Indeed, so reliant was Russell on Matt that he once refused to go on camera unless his aide was present. In despair, the managing director of MTV had to go and find him, much to Matt's embarrassment. Increasingly, as Russell's drug problems escalated, it was becoming Matt's job to try to hold Russell's life together.

In his personal life, Russell had been enjoying a rare period of stability with his girlfriend Amanda. But when she returned home to Ibiza, Russell found it impossible to be faithful. Now he was on MTV, it was even easier to pick up willing partners.

Lap dancers, though, were a particular favourite. He saw a German lap dancer for a few weeks after chatting her up on the tube. She was in her early twenties, with brown hair and a beautiful face. She was hardly an intellectual match – her main topic of conversation was her intention to have a boob enlargement. After a late-night furious row, Russell threw her out of the flat. As he ranted and raved on the doorstep, the door then shut behind him and he found himself locked out in the communal hallway – completely naked. Luckily, he found a pink umbrella in an umbrella stand, and used it to cover his modesty so he could make it to a nearby gay bar, where they lent him a pair of dirty overalls.

There was more mayhem when Russell and Matt were dispatched to Ibiza to film *Dance Floor Chart*. They would be out clubbing and filming until dawn, and then sleep until five in the evening. Off the leash, Russell was like a schoolboy in a sweet shop. There was no shortage of young clubbers ready and willing to go back to his hotel room. More often than not, the detritus of his drug use was everywhere: spent matches, tobacco, and scorched pieces of tinfoil he used for heating the heroin. Eventually, he was thrown out of his hotel room for trashing it.

Russell's only option was to share a bed with Matt. Used to the company of a female in his bed and with a rampant sex drive, Russell stirred in the middle of the night and forgot that, for once, he didn't have a woman lying next to him. He dreamily nuzzled up to his companion and caressed his bottom. Gruffly, Matt barked: 'You idiot. What are you doing?' Waking with a start, Russell said, 'Oh God! Sorry!' and went back to sleep.

On the same trip, Russell realized at 2 a.m. that he had run out of the foil he needed to prepare his fix. After Matt helpfully suggested that Russell 'go without', he agreed to assist his friend by pretending to the hotel reception staff that they needed to borrow some kitchen foil to make a 'reflector' for the shoot the next day. Matt even presented them with a coat hanger bent into a circle, to prove how it could be done.

Back in England, at times there would be rows, usually over Russell's demanding behaviour. Although they rarely came to blows, on one occasion Matt grabbed Russell's hair in the back of a car. As he did so, the vehicle went over a bump and he yanked it harder than he meant to. Russell's response was to spit at him. Matt later recalled that Russell looked in the mirror afterwards, considered his reflection, and said: 'If we ever fight, don't ever hit me in the face … cos this is beautiful.'

To feed his drugs habit, Russell's evenings would be spent in the sordid netherland of London's underworld. His dealer, Gritty, operated from his flat in a Bethnal Green tower block – a place so seedy that, according to one visitor, 'at any minute you expected the Sweeney to rush in and kick the door in.' Amid the hunched-over bodies of doped-up junkies, Russell was a strange sight with his designer clothes and sunbed tan.

Another of his regular dealers was a woman who served up drugs only from her bed. Through the fug, Russell could see addicts slumped in corners or passed out in the bath. They were scenes that he would later compare to a Hogarth print.

Though Russell sometimes protested he needed to change his lifestyle, he thrived on the risk. On one visit to Gritty's to pick up some more smack, he heard shots. It was only someone shooting pellets with an air rifle, and the only damage done was some scratches to the paintwork of his cab. Yet Matt remembered that Russell wasted no time in ringing him up to relate his 'brush with death'.

Russell never injected heroin. But after smoking it, his eyes would roll back in his head. It was such an alarming sight that his friends often feared they would come back in the morning to find him dead. Afterwards, he would fall into a deep sleep.

Among the MTV bosses, suspicions were deepening that their charismatic new presenter had a serious drugs problem, but so far they had no conclusive evidence. Determined to get to the bottom of it, they saw their chance when Russell failed to show up one afternoon to present the live kids' phone-in programme *Select*. Matt was called aside. He later recalled on a 6 Music show: 'Someone came up to me and said, "We know Russell's been on heroin. Is that why he's late?"' Matt fell into the trap and simply said: 'Yeah.'

It was not the last time that Russell was to sleep through an entire show. It was fast becoming an untenable situation to have a heroin addict – one hell-bent on recreating the drug-crazed excesses of Jim Morrison – presenting an afternoon children's music programme.

Director Will Knott, who worked with Russell at the time, said: 'Russell didn't really think about how it was going to impact on other people. If you asked him why he hadn't turned up, he would just say he had taken a load of drugs and fallen asleep. It was about rock-and-roll excess. He perceived it as the way you had to behave. A lot of his legends acted in that way, like Richard Pryor. So how are you going to behave when you are in a similar situation? You draw inspiration from your heroes.'

When Russell did clock in, it was becoming more and more difficult to get a word in edgeways, no matter how famous you were. Part of his job on *Select* was to interview celebrities, but increasingly these meetings were turning into one-sided Russell Brand monologues. 'Hear'Say, Liberty X, Mel Blatt from All Saints. I interviewed them all through a fug of crack and smack,' he later confessed to the *News of the World*. 'Half the time, I didn't understand what they were saying. I didn't even try to chat any of them up.'

One afternoon, Gritty asked Russell if he could arrange for his eight-year-old son to meet Kylie Minogue, who was due to appear on the show that day. Russell agreed, and he turned up at the studio with Gritty and the boy in tow. Giggling, Russell had already been in the loos doing drugs. Ever the professional, Kylie smiled politely. The interview later went ahead as planned, but Russell's manic and drugged-up presenting style meant that, in the end, Kylie had to sit on Russell's lap just to shut him up.

The final straw came on 12 September 2001. The day before, Russell had watched the unfolding terror in the US with a group of mates. Russell had been fascinated by bin Laden for a while – and spent the day of the atrocities discussing how world politics had made the attack on America almost inevitable. Mesmerized by the mass hysteria that was now breaking out, Russell decided to push it a bit further by showing up at work in full Arab dress and a beard as the man himself, Osama bin Laden.

'I just find huge cultural events exhilarating because it seems like everyone is freaking out – something that as a drug addict you experience all the time,' he explained later in *GQ*. 'I just thought, "Now everyone's part of the chaos." Still, a stupid thing to do.' Looking back, Russell maintains he had a point: 'There's a distinction between those poor terrible people dying in those towers over there and me doing a joke about it over here. I think one function of comedy is to expose and unravel fear.'

His MTV bosses, however, were not laughing. The sense of shock on 12 September was still very raw. It might have been a suitable subject for one of Russell's outrageous stand-up shows, but as a choice of outfit for a teatime children's programme, it could not have been more tasteless. His unreliability, drug habit and total lack of judgement meant he was taken aside and told he would no longer be presenting *Select*.

Although the incident was touched on repeatedly in his stand-up and in interviews after he left rehab as an example of his excess, in those days, friends thought little of it. 'Russell never seemed to regret it, but then Russell never regrets anything,' one said.

Director Will Knott recalled: 'When I heard Russell had dressed up as Osama, my reaction was: "Of course he did!" At the time, it was an entirely natural thing for Russell to do.'

CHAPTER SEVEN

'TV HAS BEGUN!'

'The show was essentially me having a mental breakdown. But I think it's one of the few worthwhile things I've done.'

— RUSSELL ON *RE:BRAND* IN AN
INTERVIEW WITH *TIME OUT*, 2003

ussell turned to his father and confronted him. 'I hate myself, I hate myself,' he blurted out. 'I hate being alive. And one day, mate, you are going to get a phone call: "Russell's killed himself. Russell's dead." And that is going to kill my mum. You are going to take it on the chin because I don't really think you've ever really given a fuck about me.'

Shoulder to shoulder with Ron on the canvas of an East End boxing ring, all the rage Russell had bottled up against his father came out in a brutal flash of self-loathing. In a moment, the happy-go-lucky persona was laid bare as an act – revealing a suicidal boy who had never forgiven his father for leaving when he was a baby.

It is a painfully honest scene. In the episode of his confessional documentary series *Re:Brand*, Russell had set out to tackle a taboo by challenging his dad to a boxing match. Yet Ron, caught on camera and unable to take responsibility for his son's emotional scars, barely blinks. Weakly, he responds that marriages inevitably break down, and he didn't leave Russell, he left Babs. 'Bollocks, Dad,' Russell snaps. 'That's not the fucking reason you left. You left because you didn't want to deal with it.'

Officially, the idea of *Re:Brand* was 'to test public consciousness' and to take 'a challenging look at cultural taboos'. But more than that, Russell wanted to make a 'psychological *Jackass*', where he pushed himself to confront his most personal demons. While he was later to declare it the most worthwhile thing he had ever done, he also described the series as 'essentially me having a mental breakdown'.

At the start of 2002, Russell's career prospects looked bright. Despite the Osama bin Laden debacle, Russell was still regularly flying out to Ibiza to present *Dance Floor Chart* for MTV. Indeed, even immediately after the controversy there was no further fall-out. Russell seemed more troubled by an incident that had taken place in October 2001, when he was hosting his first awards show, the *Muzik* Magazine Dance Awards, with June Sarpong. Russell ended up tripping over a plant. He was later to recall it as the most humiliating happening in his career to date.

There were other seeds that were starting to take root, too. Russell had moved to top talent agency International Creative Management, which represented some of the world's biggest stars, including, at the time, Mel Gibson and Julia Roberts. The firm had a division dedicated to helping stand-up comedians make it in television. In the previous July, he had set up his own production company, called Vanity Projects; he already had his first TV series commissioned. Even though he was barely twenty-six, Russell was still in a hurry for celebrity. When he registered the company, he gave his date of birth as 4 June 1977, making him two years younger than he really was. As one of his friends remarked: 'Russell told me you had to be young to get on and it wasn't happening quickly enough for him.'

In addition, he was looking forward to making a return to acting, playing drug dealer and commune leader Merlin in Channel 4's four-part adaptation of Zadie Smith's bestselling novel *White Teeth*. If that wasn't enough to keep him busy, Russell also had a Sunday afternoon radio show on indie music station XFM lined up.

New Year's Eve had been spent with his Spanish girlfriend Amanda in their new flat. She was back in England after spending the summer season working in Ibiza. Towards the end of 2001, she had moved into the place Russell had been sharing in Hackney with his friend Dan. But Amanda wanted some privacy to see if their relationship could work. The couple found a warehouse-style apartment just off Brick Lane. Beautifully decorated throughout, it had a huge sitting room and open-plan kitchen, with plenty of space for Russell's comedy videos and computer games.

As midnight approached, Amanda revealed it was the Spanish custom to eat twelve grapes – one for each chime of the clock – for good luck. When no grapes could be found, they ended up eating M&Ms instead. It was to prove a bad omen.

Within weeks, the relationship was over. A close friend of the pair said: 'Amanda didn't like London. She didn't speak very good English and she wasn't working. She had her own projects back in Spain. She always had schemes she wanted to get on with. Even if Russell had some money, she hated sitting around the house doing nothing. She put up with a lot of Russell's behaviour and grew exasperated when he wouldn't change.'

Later, Russell would claim he was too high on drugs even to notice that Amanda had left him. 'My flatmates and girlfriend had given up trying to talk sense into me and would find me most mornings hunched over my silver foil like a deranged Gollum,' he recalled in the *Sunday Mirror*. By his own admission, he had been incapable of nurturing a relationship, and he had not been faithful.

Yet the truth was that when Amanda ended their affair, Russell was devastated, and his friends feared the worst. 'I used to think she was ideal,' says one. 'It used to give me hope that Russell was going out with her. She was so perfect for him. The stupid thing was that none of the other girls meant anything to Russell, but I don't think he could really help himself. They weren't people he was particularly interested in talking to. It was faintly ridiculous and pointless. But he loved Amanda. He had even talked about marrying her.'

In the weeks that followed, everything reminded Russell of Amanda, from the pair of jeans she had bought him to the white towelling dressing gown she had left on the back of the bathroom door. He even kept the chorizo sausage she had abandoned in the fridge as a memento of her.

Without her, his expensive new flat seemed vast. Maudlin, Russell whiled away his hours playing *Grand Theft Auto* and drowning his sorrows. Even the Sunday newspapers were a bitter reminder. When a little Spanish girl appeared on the front of the *Observer* travel section sitting on the back of a car, his MTV mate Matt undiplomatically rubbed salt in the wound, by telling him it was a picture of Amanda driving out of his life.

With Amanda gone, nothing really mattered. Russell was twenty-six, but the issues from his childhood, which had been bubbling under, were now starting to erupt and manifest themselves in a self-destructive rage.

His father Ron had noticed that his drug-taking was getting out of control. 'I lost my temper with him a couple of times. We had one furious row after a gig, which his friends had been filming, and he was all over the place. He died a death on stage. He had what he called "one ounce of cocaine and no material". He was awful and I shouted at him: "What the fuck are you doing? Get a grip," and we didn't speak for a couple of weeks. Then I gave him a phone call. It was important to keep the lines of communication open. As he got into harder drugs, his behaviour became more extreme. It was upsetting to see.'

Now Russell's need for sex was becoming almost as dangerous as his addiction to drugs. He'd found that, despite his drug use, he still had a libido. Plus, he had a cheeky, flirtatious way about him. Combined with disconcertingly direct eye contact, he could easily pull two or three women a day, just by chatting them up on the street.

'Russell was very democratic when it came to women,' recalled one friend. 'There were all sorts – black girls, white girls, East European girls – every type imaginable. Generally, though, he preferred curvier women with big breasts. Some would even stick around for a day or two and then you'd never see them again. You got the impression that it wasn't just the sex Russell wanted. Sometimes he liked having girls for the physical comfort, and he loved being mothered and fussed over. He also hated being alone.'

Yet Russell wanted a quicker fix that didn't involve the delicate mating ritual of having to seduce a new girl. With his pop-star good looks, Russell didn't need to pay for sex. But increasingly, drugs were robbing him of any moral restraints. Ever since he had slept with a hooker on holiday at the age of sixteen, Russell had not just enjoyed the convenience of prostitution, he had positively revelled in the sleaziness. He needed sex in the same way he needed a hit of heroin. Just as he visited his dealer for smack, now he visited the massage parlours of Soho. It was simply faster and more convenient. The only saving grace was that he was assiduous about using condoms.

It was typical of his risqué behaviour at this time that one night he boasted of attending an orgy in a seedy tower block in Paddington. He had hoped for an X-rated version of a Turkish Delight ad, only to find cheap nibbles set out on paper plates with balloons attached. As he later remarked: 'It was like an orgy directed by Mike Leigh.'

As his sexual activity peaked, Russell claimed he was sleeping with around five women a day. 'One in the morning, maybe two for lunch and three for tea,' as he later told GQ. 'Then someone might stick around all night. A good week would be at least twenty in various configurations.' He would admit it was a very empty feeling going up the stairs and seeing the punter before him coming down the other way. A colleague from the time recalled: 'Russell could definitely shag. He would disappear at lunchtimes. He just liked to have sex with anyone. He didn't need to pay prostitutes. He just liked it.'

On one occasion, Russell dragged Matt along to a brothel, telling him to sit there and have a cup of tea while he had a quickie. Russell disappeared into a room while Matt was left watching *Who Wants to Be a Millionaire?* and making small talk with a prostitute in a dressing gown on the sofa. Minutes later, Russell came running out, saying he had changed his mind. In hot pursuit was one very angry overweight hooker, who complained that Russell hadn't even given her a chance. The boys' exit came as no surprise to the elderly madam on the door, who remarked: 'We thought when you two came in you wanted the gay sauna next door.'

Meanwhile, Russell was busy on the work front, too. He had an original concept for a new programme: a mix of animation, some live performance and some stunt TV. Produced with his close friend Martino Sclavi, the pilot was nothing if not ambitious. By sheer force of personality, Russell had already managed to attract interest from fledgling cable channel Play UK. Most of their output was comedy repeats like *The Fast Show* and *Goodness Gracious Me*. But the station did have a budget for original programming. When Russell went for a meeting with the channel's commissioners, he surpassed himself by standing on the desk, dropping his trousers and letting off a fire extinguisher. When the show got commissioned anyway, it confirmed to Russell that bad behaviour got results.

The budget was £250,000 for ten programmes. As Russell was a newcomer who had only just set up his own production company, the plan was for a well-known firm called Vera Productions to supervise the series and oversee it through to completion. Established by comedian Rory Bremner, Vera had lots of experience making programmes with an anarchic edge, including shows by comedy terrorist Mark Thomas. Geoff

Atkinson was put in overall charge. A successful writer and producer, Geoff had racked up credits on every major comedy programme from *The Two Ronnies* to *Spitting Image*. Thankfully for Russell, he was also a firm believer in putting creativity before commercialism. He was a genial, good-tempered man with a lively sense of humour, and he was to need every last ounce of it.

Geoff recalled: 'Russell just sent a tape in cold. It was a bit like a showreel. It was ambitious, to put it mildly. At that time, Russell was on the fringes of TV and doing bits and bobs and still flying out to Spain to do stuff for MTV. He wasn't known and he wasn't unknown either. But the idea for the format kept changing. That was a worry because if you are on a slim budget, then you have to be pretty clear what you are going to do. Eventually, we narrowed it down. Russell would go out on the road in a bus and discover things.'

Based in his own office at Vera's West End headquarters, Russell was in his element. He persuaded his two mates from MTV, Matt Morgan and Will Knott, to come over and join him. With his friends around him, a quarter-of-a-million-pound budget and a creative free hand, he was in a strong position to create the programme he wanted. But Russell's primary aim seemed to be to create chaos, and get it captured on camera. As Will later observed: 'To this day, I don't know how we got away with it. It's never happened before and I don't suppose it will ever happen again.'

As Russell saw it, the idea of a trip round Britain would be like 'Shaggy and his gang going on an adventure in the Scooby bus'. Interviews were lined up with various fringe groups and eccentrics around the country. They would be cut with reality footage of life with Russell, Will and Matt driving around. At vast cost, a Winnebago, complete with onboard shower and loo, was hired and stocked with a fortnight's food.

Finally, after weeks of preparation, all they needed to do

was collect some belongings from Will's flat in Notting Hill. Russell, who had been away filming for MTV, was to meet them there. First stop was Cornwall, where they were due to quiz the Cornish separatists.

It was only 9 a.m. But as Russell loomed into view, it was clear that he had had more for breakfast than just a bowl of cereal. He was swaggering down the road, waving a bottle of gin, shouting: 'I am here. TV has begun!' It was the first time Russell had seen the bus. When he noticed it had a ladder attached to the back, he immediately conjured up an image of himself 'surfing' around Britain on top of it. He climbed up and insisted the cameras started rolling.

One by one, the crew tried to persuade Russell to come down. His friend Martino, who was supposed to be producing the show, was reduced to tears. The director, Will, told Russell he would get points on his licence if he so much as moved an inch with Russell on the roof. Matt just laughed at the absurdity of it all.

Suspecting that things might get out of hand, Vera had taken the precaution of sending one of their own people along, a producer called Duncan. When Duncan demanded that he come down, Russell viewed him as a killjoy who was asking him to compromise his principles of making great television. So, dangling himself over the edge, Russell stuck his fingers down his throat – and threatened to vomit on him. 'At that point, all hell broke loose,' said Will. 'The executives back at the office were called. Russell insisted that all he wanted to do was make good telly. They were having none of it. The whole shoot was canned then and there.'

Two hours later, Russell was already regretting what he had done. He drowned his sorrows in the pub with Matt, and admitted he couldn't understand why he – or 'we', as he preferred to put it – had acted so childishly. 'It will be okay,' he said, in a bid to reassure himself as much as anyone else. 'Let's just not tell our mums.'

After Christmas, in spring 2002, the bosses relented and the show was back on track. There was still no concept for the programme, which was to go through three more incarnations before making it to the screen. The only theme seemed to be that it featured Russell behaving outrageously. As Matt later recalled: 'Russell thought anything he did would make good television. It was: "Put the camera on me – that's telly!"'

Indeed, Russell was constantly on a quest to create a happening out of the most mundane event. When he spotted a pensioner in the street, he insisted they follow her into her sheltered housing block. 'She didn't know why we were there,' said Matt. 'The buzzer gate was left open. She was saying: "I don't know if you are meant to be in here." Russell was saying: "Let's look at your house and how you live!" She was shitting herself. He was saying: "Look at her – she's telly!"'

With no one really sure what the series was about, it also went through various title changes. At one point, Russell wanted to name the show *It Was At That Time That I Realized That The Thing I Had Created Was Truly Evil*. He didn't care it was a bit of a mouthful. He argued that it could be boiled down to an acronym: *IWATTTIRTTTIHCWTE*. When it was pointed out to Russell that people couldn't say that either, Russell insisted: 'But it will look funny in the *TV Times*!'

Regardless of opposition from both Matt and Will, Russell even wanted to sing the theme tune. After opening with a scratching noise, Russell planned to kick off an indecipherable white-boy Ali-G-style rap. Then, over an ambient melody, Russell would pipe up again – this time in his best camped-up Hammer Horror voice – saying: 'It was at that time that I realized that the thing I had created was truly ev-il. Tru-ly ev-il. Truly evil.'

For despite Russell's disastrous audition for boy band 5ive, he was still toying with the idea of getting into music, although he seemed unable to record anything that wasn't utterly absurd. Among his other offerings were 'I'm A Baby

With A Beard' and 'Hong Kong Kicky Boots'. He even talked about filling in as the frontman with the Blockheads after Ian Dury died. He attended a recording session, but – as far as the band remember – did not lay down any tracks. However, Russell's presumptuous belief that he could replace the legendary singer was later to become a running joke with Matt.

As Russell rampaged round the country with a camera in tow, back at Vera's headquarters, Geoff was having to deal with the fallout. Russell was then going through a phase of dropping his trousers at every available opportunity. At various times and for various reasons, Geoff had complaints from female members of Vera's office staff, the organizers of London Fashion Week, and even publicist Max Clifford, after Russell launched a comedy terror raid on his offices with his drug dealer Gritty.

Geoff said: 'In terms of grief for the office, it was immense. There was a high price to pay. I think Russell wanted to be Mark Thomas. But in fact Mark is incredibly rigorous and you always know why he's doing it and the reasons. With *Re:Brand*, basically, if the phone didn't ring and someone was annoyed, you wondered what was going on.

'I knew if you said to Russell, "Don't do it," he would be like a naughty child and do it more. So I would say to him: "I want to understand what it is you are trying to achieve. If I understand where you are trying to get to, then maybe I could help you. But if you go and annoy people because that's what you think makes great television, then you are wrong. You will just look like a prat." To his credit, Russell understood that. He plays the game of being a sort of outsider, but there is a bit of Russell which is very focused.'

Geoff was also prepared to put up with a lot because he felt Russell was such a presence on screen. 'A bit like David Frost, he was made for television. On screen, he's big, but not so big that he's annoying. Then, suddenly, he can get quite intimate.'

It was Will, the series director, who got the project back on course, according to Geoff. Will really believed in Russell, but also refused to let Russell mess him around. Geoff says: 'There was litter all over the place early on. So you needed someone who was anchored enough, like Will, to be able to deliver, and know what a half-hour of television needed to look like.'

For Russell, the show was an excuse to sink to new lows of depravity. Often, he would come up with a concept for a programme and quickly change his mind. For one idea, one of many that never saw the light of day, Russell wanted to explore the fetishistic world of adults who get a sexual thrill from being treated like infants. Russell bought an adult nappy from a costume shop, and Matt filmed a woman spanking Russell on the bottom with a carpet-beater and applying clothes pegs to his genitals. In the middle of it, Russell was appalled to see Matt was so bored by the iniquity that he had stopped filming and was busy texting one of his mates instead. The next day, for a laugh, Russell dressed up as a policeman on camera to ring up the woman, asking if she had been approached by two maniacs who claimed to be making a documentary. She confessed she had.

For another episode, Russell was reunited with an ex-girlfriend to explore ways that their relationship may have gone wrong. But it only reopened old wounds. Russell and the girl spent so much time in the bedroom arguing that Will and Matt eventually went home and left them to it.

Russell managed to combine business with pleasure by filming a segment in his drug dealer Gritty's East End crack house. He created an alternative society, set in the future, where drugs had been legalized. They even hired renowned feng shui expert Paul Darby to come down for the day and provide a makeover for Gritty's crack den. 'That never went anywhere either,' recalled Will. 'We were just randomly filming things and then forgetting about them. We also had an idea to go back to Russell's school, but they changed their minds when they remembered who he was. In our haphazard way, we were just going to turn up and hope something worked out. We did a lot of that in those days.'

Russell had always been fascinated by the concept of anarchy and creating new world orders and societies. He had been twenty-two when he attended his first demonstration. He was on his way to buy a pair of trainers, when a group of masked anarchists entered his tube carriage. He decided to join them. He had never seen a sit-down protest before. When he spotted police trying to drag away a woman on the ground, he gallantly interjected: 'At least let her stand up first.' Looking at Russell as though he was a total idiot, the woman hissed: 'I don't want to stand. That's the point!'

When anarchists, eco-warriors and hunt saboteurs, as well as other groups such as cyclists, anti-fur activists and even prostitutes, converged on London on 1 May 2002, Russell decided it was too good an opportunity to miss.

Will, in particular, was reluctant. 'I just didn't want to do it. I couldn't see a programme in it, just wandering about in a riot. It was rubbish in terms of TV production because there was no story there. But it was easier just to go and film Russell and show him the film afterwards, so he could see it for himself. That was easier than trying to talk him out of it. The only thing that Russell wanted to do was lark about. He was particularly keen at that period of time on taking his clothes off at any opportunity.'

It was the height of the protest and 1,000 demonstrators, who had marched down New Bond Street, were involved in a stand-off in Piccadilly with several hundred police officers. As it promised to be the main flashpoint of the day, Russell made sure he was right in the thick of it. First, he borrowed a giant rubber phallus from the International Union of Sex Workers and waved it in front of police. Next, he managed to break through a ring of officers surrounding the statue of Eros and climb to the top.

It was an exhilarating sight to see the heaving masses below staring up at him. Unsure of what to do next, Russell took off his T-shirt and announced he was stripping for socialism. When he got down to his Y-fronts, officers warned him he would be arrested if he went any further. It was all the encouragement he needed. He yanked his pants down, punched both fists in the air in short-lived triumph, and was wrestled to the ground. To prolong the spectacle, he pretended to be an epileptic having a fit. He was dragged away screaming he had lost his identity bracelet.

There was no doubt that Russell was the star protester of the day, particularly as he was an MTV presenter. For a while, Russell even had some fleeting fame among anarchists. Asked by journalists why he had done it, Russell gave a variety of different answers, ranging from 'Armageddon' to 'Revolution'.

'It was a moment of madness to show you can do something to change your life,' he told waiting reporters. The reality was that he thought it would make good TV. Still, just in case he hadn't got enough footage, he was arrested a second time in Soho a few hours later, for being naked on top of a TV satellite van and waving a red flag.

After a lot of false starts, *Re:Brand* began to come together. For each episode, Russell would challenge himself to confront a taboo. Because they now had so few filming days, the subject had to be something that was both edgy and comic. Will recalled: 'In all, there were four attempts to make the show – and only the last one made it on to screen. Finally, we decided that we would come up with some stupidly simplistic, naïve idea and then the programme would be an exploration of us realizing we were twats.'

On screen, Russell was charming, engaging and compelling. But off screen, he could be moody and difficult, prone to aggression. When he did get into fights, he later said that his first instinct was to perplex his opponent with comments like: 'Come on, princess, do you want to dance around my garden?' Just as he had in the programme where he fought Ron, Russell often talked about what would happen if he killed himself. 'It was a concept he liked playing with at that time,' said Will. 'I don't think any of us really took it seriously.'

'It was the alcohol, not the heroin, that was the problem,' recalled another former colleague. 'He was fine on the heroin. It would just make him a little bit dazed. Everyone knew he had a smack habit. He could cope with all the drugs – except one. The alcohol. You would meet him at nine o'clock in the morning and he'd be pissed because he'd had three cans of Special Brew. Then he would drink on set. Because he had done MTV and he'd always been pissed, I think he felt that if he had to put in any kind of performance, he needed to be pissed.

'He had a great mind and was a very clever person. He loved comedy and he loved to use situations and go off on a tangent. The problem with Russell was that he was not disciplined. At that point, he couldn't structure his mind and he had this incredible ego. There were quite a lot of tantrums and aggressive behaviour. To be fair, I think that was the worst of him. He was going through a nervous breakdown and also pushing himself as well. He wanted to put himself through personally difficult journeys. We all have demons inside, but when Russell drank, he really let them loose. It was as if Russell wanted to push himself over the edge.'

On one occasion, when he had been due to attend a meeting, Russell told the team he would see them in five minutes. Instead, he took a detour to meet up with Gritty at his house – and stayed there for three days.

Will remembers: 'There were a few times when he would turn up in the morning and he had done a bit of H. I would say: "Oh, Russell, you look like shit. Think what you are going to look like on screen. I don't really care what you do, but it doesn't look fantastic on telly." When he took heroin, he would be really dopey and not animated. He would be delivering the lines, but in a kind of utilitarian way. But I think it wasn't as bad as all that. It wasn't the sort of hell that people like to believe it was.'

Instead, it was what was going on in Russell's head that caused the most damage. 'Russell was going through a hard time,' says Geoff. 'It both helped and hindered him. He was doing what he had to do and I do think the shows he did were fantastic. But what he also did was put himself on the line. That was the brave thing, but it also made him vulnerable. This was therapy for him in a strange way. It wasn't like he was just completely out of control, but the demons were hanging around.'

That was also the impression of veteran English actress Wendy Danvers, who appeared in an episode of *Re:Brand* with Russell, in which he set about exploring his attitude to sex in old age.

Wendy was invited to go on a 'dirty weekend' with Russell to Eastbourne. What she found was a lost boy who asked her to sew on his buttons for him, and who was constantly on the phone to his mum. 'I had been warned before by other members of the crew that he could be a bit grand and difficult, but I didn't find him like that at all. I was told that if he didn't like you, then you had problems. But I loved him. He was over the top, but in a harmless way. There was something very vulnerable about him that made you want to give him a big hug.'

It was obvious that Russell was living on the edge. 'His brain was moving so quickly,' added Wendy. 'He was always getting what you were saying, before you'd even said it. He seemed to let himself go and anything would come out. He was pushing himself to extremes. You can knock down all the boundaries, but then you feel a bit lost. That was how it seemed with Russell. If I had found out he had gone mad, I would not have been surprised.'

Russell and Wendy had many heart-to-hearts and stayed in touch after the show. He would confide in her that what he really wanted was a long-term relationship. 'He told me he was sick of all the models, and he wanted a girlfriend "not in the business" to settle down with. When he rang me afterwards, I would always ask him if he had found a nice girl. It struck me that going to brothels was his way of getting the best value and being in control. With prostitutes, it was the easiest way for Russell to get his fantasies played out without having to coax or cajole. During the show, when we talked about sex, the idea which upset him most was that I wasn't interested in sex any more. It was almost as if he couldn't conceive a time when he wouldn't be interested in sex.'

By early summer 2002, tensions were coming to a head, in particular between Russell and producer Sean Grundy, who had been brought in to keep an eye on the production. The concept of the latest episode was that Russell would be shown how to be gay. The culmination was a visit to a gay pub, in which Russell would see if he could pick up a homosexual man and masturbate him.

It was perhaps the toughest challenge of all. Russell spent most of the show in a state of manic hysteria. 'He was incredibly tense about the whole thing,' said a colleague. 'It was an idea he came up with, but he was scared. When there were technical problems and the radio mikes didn't work, Russell flew into a rage in the back of a cab. Sean said to Russell: "Will you just shut the fuck up and let me get these sorted?" Russell turned back to him and said: "What the fuck did you say to me?" and then took a swing. The pair of them ended up fighting, until the taxi driver stopped and pulled them both out.'

Will remembers the day well. 'I was in the edit [suite] and I got this call from Matt, who was saying: "Get the fuck down here. They are fighting in the car. Russell's hissing at him." I don't think it was anything to do with Russell being tense about the gay stuff. They had just fallen out.'

If the exercise proved anything, it confirmed that Russell was a heterosexual. To reassert his masculinity after the incident, he hired a limo and picked up two prostitutes. The final shot shows one of them sticking her stiletto heel up his bottom.

For the episode 'Homeless James', Russell invited a hobo and drug addict he had met on the street to stay at his house. James would beg at the Barclays cashpoint close to the Vera offices. When Russell had seen him being hassled by police, he had intervened and they had stayed friendly.

It is uncomfortable, but compelling viewing. It is hard not to flinch as Russell takes off all his clothes and gets in the bath with James, berates him for touching his penis by accident with his foot, and calls him 'his little homeless dolly'. For his part, James seems both touched and traumatized by the attention.

'What I loved about that was that in the end nothing got sorted out,' says Geoff. 'Russell didn't really want James in his flat and James didn't really want to be there. That's much better than having an easy ending. I think television tends to think it has to sort things out.'

Yet there was to be a personal cost. Russell had been doing his XFM show with Will and Matt on Sunday lunchtimes for about four months at this time. When it coincided with having homeless James in his flat, Russell decided to take James with him and put him on air. To cap it off, he read out some pornographic letters, prompting a discussion about anal sex.

While they were on air, the phone rang. Will remembers: 'It was the station controller telling us: "Once you've finished your show, you are out of here." We tried everything. We even got Russell's mum to ring up and say that we were naughty boys to try and calm it down, but it didn't work.'

Though the *Re:Brand* episodes that made it on air were riveting, confessional and original, the best episode never even saw the light of day, according to Geoff. Russell had gone up to Norfolk to stay for a week in the house of a heroin-addicted prostitute and her partner and their young daughter. Russell's thesis was that you could not have sex with a prostitute if you got to know her.

Geoff continued: 'Russell went up there to see if he could sleep with her, given all these things. The programme starts with you thinking: "I am really going to hate these people." But you came away with enormous sympathy. What came through was that the mother really did care for the child, even though she was a prostitute taking heroin. The conventional wisdom would be to take the child out of the situation, but the programme showed it isn't as simple as that. Because it was Russell, he managed to get something that was really quite unusual from it. The people really opened up to him. It was one of the best things I have ever seen. Afterwards, I remember phoning Russell and saying: "This is fantastic. I am so proud of what you've done."' The show was never aired after the mother changed her mind and would not allow the child to be identified.

The episode also taught Russell a lesson: not only about prostitutes, but also about the effect that using people's lives for TV can have on them. In an interview with *The Word* magazine, he later said: 'They were junkies and we'd use, totally off our heads together. Her husband and her husband's brother used to pimp her. They would be out trying to drum up business and scoring drugs and she'd be upstairs with a punter; you could hear them fucking upstairs. We'd be looking after their little daughter, their little girl. It was mental.'

At the end of his week-long stay, Russell decided to put the premise to the test. 'I goes: "Here's fifty quid, let's fuck." Her husband, this withered, pinched junkie of a man, nice bloke, though, really, just cried. And cried. "I trusted you, I thought you were friends." I had to go: "It was just an experiment, a show!" I didn't do it.'

In the middle of all the chaos, Russell was also filming his role as Merlin in Channel 4's adaptation of *White Teeth*. For a method actor who was a heavy drug user, the part of the spaced-out commune leader was a gift. The drama was even set in Willesden, where Russell had lived during his student days. His most important scene called on him to host an end-of-the-world party that turns into an orgy. The shoot involved early starts and Russell spent a lot of time sitting around in trailers, but for once the filming passed without incident. Although he received only passing mentions in reviews, Russell put in a good performance filled with unusual nuances.

Starting on 26 August 2002, *Re:Brand* was broadcast at 11.15 p.m. and then repeated at 1.50 a.m. on digital channel Play UK. In a late time slot on a struggling cable channel, few people saw it. One episode, about Russell's visit to the leader of the Young BNP, recorded zero viewers.

Those who saw it, liked it, however. One comment on the station's website said: '*Re:Brand* was out of this world. Totally honest, unique TV from a bloke who isn't afraid to confront things.' Generally, though, the show went virtually unnoticed. Only TV reviewer Dominik Diamond in the *Daily Star* remarked on it, calling it 'the most original show I've seen in the last five years'.

A month later, Play UK folded due to poor ratings. Russell had hoped that because the programme had been commissioned by a cable channel, it would gather viewers from repeats. Now the show was filed away and forgotten about. In the end, Russell had bared his soul, but for very little in return.

After *Re:Brand* finished, Russell fell out with Will. The director explained: 'Russell said he wanted a producer's credit. I said, "I can't really give you that because you haven't really produced it." He got well uppity about that. We were in Bella Pasta – and he just burst into tears. It was awful, but it was out of my hands. I couldn't invent credits. But Russ and I made it up soon after.'

Geoff said: 'When the series finally ended, most people felt that Russell needed time and space to sort things out. I was very proud of *Re:Brand*, but we paid a price and so did Russell.

'Even at his worst, it wasn't like you wanted to kill Russell. You just wanted to show him how to get it together and emerge as a reasonable human being.'

CHAPTER EIGHT

BURNING BRIDGES

'They told me if I didn't stop doing drugs, I'd be dead, in prison or a mental home within six months.'

— RUSSELL BRAND IN THE *SUNDAY MIRROR*, REMEMBERING 2002

When Russell got a part in the BBC Christmas comedy special, *Cruise of the Gods*, it should have been the dream gig. Not only was he working with comedians he admired – Steve Coogan, David Walliams and Rob Brydon – but the show was also filmed onboard a luxury cruise liner as it sailed around the Aegean.

Essentially a satire on *Star Trek* conventions, the ninety-minute comedy-drama told the story of Andy van Allan. Rob Brydon, of *Marion and Geoff* fame, played the role of the faded star of fictional cult eighties sci-fi series *Children of Caster*. In desperation, he agrees to be a guest celebrity onboard a fan cruise. Meanwhile, he has to deal with the fact that his original co-star, Nick Lee (portrayed by Steve Coogan), has since shot to fame in the US. Russell was to play one of the sci-fi show's fanatical fans.

While Russell insists he didn't risk taking drugs onboard, he did hit the booze. By the end of the first week, Russell's antics had included dangling himself over the edge of the liner in an effort to impress one of the cabaret dancers he fancied. Matters got even worse when the ship was in dock. In Istanbul, he was involved in a fight in a lap-dancing club. In Athens, he had yet another punch-up in a brothel.

After just one week, Russell was fired. Fearing how he would react if they sacked him in a confined space, the producers got him off the boat to make sure he was a safe distance away before they broke the news. As Russell later recalled to *Time Out*'s

Malcolm Hay: 'I was delivered to the airport like a vet-bound hound who believes he's en route to a sumptuous country run.' According to another version of the story, Russell was shipped off by speedboat into the hands of waiting police, and then texted the news as the cruise ship sailed off into the sunset.

Whatever the truth, getting the sack gave Russell cause to reflect. This wasn't the opinion of punters who just didn't get his comedy routine. This was the opinion of people he respected. In particular, Russell was a huge admirer of Steve Coogan. In his drive to become the best comic he could be, he had watched the Alan Partridge shows again and again to pick up tips on delivery and timing. Moreover, Coogan's company Baby Cow had also produced the show.

No one was more pleased to see Russell leave the shoot than future *Little Britain* star David Walliams. Years later, the comedian told Russell: 'I hated you when I first met you. I was so pleased when you were sacked. I thought, "Good, because you are ruining the whole production."'

The finished product was shown on 23 December 2002. In the final edit, Russell made it on to the screen for no more than five seconds. With a black woolly hat pulled down tight over his head, Russell's only line was to ask Rob Brydon's character about a minor plot discrepancy he had spotted in the sci-fi series.

Back at home in his flat off Brick Lane, Russell was now forced to take a long, hard look at himself. He could no longer ignore the fact that he was becoming unemployable. In total despair, he wandered the streets of the East End in the rain, realizing that his TV career was heading for the wall.

Neither could he take comfort from the fact that his stand-up was going well. He had long ago stopped bothering to rehearse his material. Instead, he thrived on the adrenalin of getting himself in trouble, and then being able to talk his way out of it. Increasingly, audiences were no longer laughing.

At one gig, Russell was so short of material that he resorted to covering a Barbie doll with a condom and stuffing it up his bottom, claiming he was making a point about false ideals of beauty. The appalled audience sat there shell-shocked, until one heckler finally thought of something to say and shouted out: 'You're gay!'

To make up for his dearth of material, Russell would resort to his old shock tactics. He would go to the butcher's and buy a pig's head to use as a puppet. His mate Matt would also be roped in to add to the absurd atmosphere, and be told to sit in silence in the audience with pigs' trotters sticking out of his sleeves.

Confrontational and aggressive, the gigs were now turning violent. 'There is nothing sadder or lonelier than standing there wanting to be adored, but receiving instead just disdain and even hatred,' recalled Russell years later in an interview with *GQ*. 'But I would turn up, off my head, having prepared no material and find this audience sitting there demanding to be entertained. And the only way I could think to entertain them was to behave very badly.

'I remember planting homeless people outside a theatre, asking them to beg people for money as they went inside. Then I dragged the homeless people in off the street and asked them to reveal how much money the audience had given them. And it wasn't funny so much as very uncomfortable for everyone.'

Indeed, Russell was pushing every single boundary. Despite his vegetarian beliefs, he would buy dead birds and mice, line them up on the stage, smash them with a hammer and then throw them at the audience. 'I was about to kick this squashed chick into the audience, and this bloke said, "If that hits me, I'm going to come and kill you,"' Russell told comedy website Chortle. 'And I was scared, but figured that I couldn't back down, so I kicked it right at him and it landed on his lapel. He came up on the stage – a great big geezer – and grabbed me by the throat and started marching me to the back of the stage. And there was a goat's head on the front of the stage, and he picked it up and went to strike me on the head with this goat's head. I didn't know what to do, so I said, "Mate, it's all just a joke, help me introduce the second act. Ladies and gentlemen ..." He just sort of forgot what he was doing and started applauding.' At other times, Russell would buy locusts and throw them into the audience. His comic justification was that it would be a welcome burst of 'chaos' in their mundane lives.

The fog of drugs made Russell both defensive and aggressive. During one gig, Russell took particular exception to a persistent heckler in the crowd. Again, he badly misjudged the situation. He pulled the man up on to the stage, only to find he was mentally ill.

Worst of all, he was also starting to burn bridges in the place that was his comedy spiritual home, the Edinburgh Fringe. The arson had started the summer before. Turning up at the Late 'n' Live club at the Gilded Balloon with no gags and no rehearsal in August 2001, he almost caused a riot.

Known as the comedian's playground, the club started at 1 a.m. and was the toughest possible arena for a stand-up. Only the best survived it. At previous high-octane gigs, Phil Kay had climbed up on to a balcony and nearly broken his neck. Johnny Vegas had once been pulled off stage by five other comedians, when it was decided his set had gone on too long.

At the time, Russell was spending half the week in Ibiza filming *Dance Floor Chart*. He flew in for a week to do the Edinburgh Fringe. He had no material, so he went to a joke shop and bought some fake blood bags for some comedy stunts. Anticipating he might not get a good reception, he also took the precaution of getting one of the street souvenir-sellers to fashion a metal sign for the evening, which read:

'Fuck off Late 'n' Live.' He planned to produce it as soon as he got heckled.

Barefoot, and wearing a white vest with the blood packs sellotaped to his body, Russell went on the stage that night. For the first thirty seconds, he stood there and said absolutely nothing. When the baying started, Russell asked: 'Oh, do you want more drama?' He invited the audience to throw things at him, downed the glass of vodka he was holding, smashed it, and used the shard to stab the blood bags. The crowd went wild, hurling every missile they could find at the stage. By now, there was broken glass on the floor. Russell's hard-man act was somewhat ruined by the fact that in his shoeless state he had to tiptoe round it to get off stage. Eventually, he had to be ushered out the back of the building with the help of comedian Sean Hughes. When they bumped into each other several weeks later, Russell couldn't even remember meeting him.

Yet one friend who witnessed the performance felt that Russell was not as out of control as he liked to make out. 'It took Russell quite a lot of preparation to get blood capsules and the other props. He had given it some thought. Despite all the chaos that surrounded him, I sometimes wondered if Russell knew exactly what he was doing. It was like controlled self-destruction. It was as if he had to find out how low he could sink before coming back up again.'

A year later, fellow comedian Matt Blaize remembers bumping into Russell at the Fringe at eleven in the morning. 'He was marching along in this trance. I said: "Alright, Russell." He was like: "Alright, Matt, didn't see you there!" He told me he had just been over to this whorehouse. I was like: "Russell, what the hell are you doing fucking whores at this time of the morning?" He was living in his own world of vice and seediness. But sad as it was, it made you laugh.'

The gig to end all gigs was when Russell hosted *So You Think You're Funny?* in August 2002. The prestigious competition, also held at the Gilded Balloon, was one of comedy's most important talent contests. Past winners had included Rhona Cameron and Peter Kay. Russell himself had taken part in 2000, getting to the final nine.

Saturday 17 August was also the day of the arrests of Ian Huntley and Maxine Carr for the Soham murders. For weeks, the nation had been consumed by the horrific story of how schoolgirls Holly Wells and Jessica Chapman had been abducted and murdered. Now there was general shock that the school handyman and his girlfriend were in the frame for the killings.

Out of his mind on a mixture of heroin and Smirnoff Ice, and stripped naked to the waist, Russell turned on the punters that night, proclaiming: 'You killed them little girls!' The idea, he later claimed, had been to make a complex point about how the whole of society was culpable for child murders. However noble his aims, several members of the audience did not appreciate the accusation and threatened to beat him up.

Rob Rouse, the next comedian up on stage, tried his best to lighten the mood, assuring the crowd: 'Russell's comedy is terrific if you're on heroin.' Failing to take the hint, Russell returned, flashed his penis and threw a bottle. To Russell's fury, the stage manager then turned off the microphone. Besieged by boos and cries of 'Off! Off!' and unable to make himself heard, Russell was apoplectic with rage. In a dramatic exit, he clambered through the audience using empty chairs as stepping stones, shouting, 'None of you are fit to hear my jokes!'

Even that wasn't the end of the evening. As the security team surrounded him, Russell tried to pull some of them down the stairwell with him, until finally the head of security got him in a headlock. As he was carried out, he kicked out at the plate-glass door, getting a serious laceration that went right to the bone. According to one eyewitness: 'At this point, most people would have gone home and thought, "Bad night!" Oh no, Russell repeatedly tried to get back in with a gashed leg, shouting and yelling: "You are all cunts!"'

With blood pulsing out of his shin, Russell was arrested for criminal damage to the door. He was rushed to the Edinburgh Royal Infirmary by ambulance and doctors told him if the cut had been an inch to the left, he could have lost his leg altogether. He was given 100 stitches – and warned he would be left with a huge scar. But even from his hospital stretcher, Russell's main concern was where he could score his next hit. He beckoned over some teenage boys, and gave them £40 to go and buy some heroin. Not surprisingly, he never saw them again.

Among the audience that night had been the venue's director, Karen Koren. Probably the most respected figure on the Edinburgh comedy scene, Karen had long had a soft spot for Russell, after spotting his talent at the Hackney Empire New Act of the Year show in 2000. She had championed him ever since.

This time, however, he had gone too far. Russell was kept in hospital overnight and the next morning phoned Karen from the ward, to tell her he would be in late. Appalled by what she had seen, Karen told him he was a maniac who could not be trusted to perform at the Gilded Balloon again. Russell then wrote her 'a beautiful letter', according to Karen, in which he admitted his behaviour had been a disgrace. Drugged up on painkillers and deeply depressed, Russell caught the train home to London.

Looking back at the incident, Karen said: 'In those days, Russell didn't want to go on and be funny. He wanted to go on and be shocking. Russell was a comedian who went on stage not knowing what he was going to say. Phil Kay never went on stage knowing what he was going to say either. But he had a kinder, warmer, deeper character than Russell. Russell had an angry personality because of his childhood. The comments about Holly and Jessica weren't a joke. It was Russell being angry. That was his persona. On stage, Russell would be saying: "Fuck you, bastards!" And that's not funny. If you were as angry as Russell, the drugs only made it worse.

'That night at Late 'n' Live, I was annoyed at him for not taking his job seriously and for being unprofessional – Russell was supposed to be the host – although I also thought the situation was badly handled. You can cause a riot if you interfere too much and my technician turned off the mike while Russell was ranting and raving. She shouldn't have done that because that made him angrier. And he started throwing the mike and screaming and shouting.'

Russell had already been advised by his management company that throwing dead animals at the audience was unlikely to set him on the path to stardom. As Russell's descent escalated, and he continued to fail to get help for his problems, they parted company.

By now, word had spread in comedy circles that Russell was a junkie heading for a meltdown, or worse. 'It's a small scene and Russell's sacking by his agents was the talk of the industry,' recalls one old friend and comedy veteran. 'Russell was only twenty-seven, but he had already burned virtually every bridge in the business. No agent would touch him and his career was virtually over. He was this massive delicious car crash that you just loved watching, to see what he would do next. You knew he was going to end up dead and no one was going to do or say anything about it.

'I mean, you would turn up to important industry parties and Russell would be smoking heroin in the toilets for anyone who was anyone in the comedy business to see. What are you going to do when someone wants to wreck their life that badly? Most people have one addiction – a lifetime thing that really fucks them up and eventually kills them. Russell had four or five. At that point, there seemed no way that Russell was going to see thirty. There was nothing anyone could do about it. You were seeing him self-destruct. But you had to stand by and watch it happen because you can't help anyone until they help themselves.'

Others felt that the drugs were the symptom rather than the cause of Russell's problems. 'You would piece together whatever information you knew about Russell and that didn't really make sense. He had a really close relationship with his mum and his dad really loved him. I mean, half the country has grown up with one parent, so no one could figure out why Russell couldn't get over his childhood.

'Who knew where the drugs ended and Russell began? I thought the drugs were more a desperation to make the fame work. Russell had wanted to be famous from the day he was born. He had a terrible fear of failure and he wanted to be as big as his heroes, Richard Pryor and Bill Hicks. He probably had a nervous breakdown because *Re:Brand* didn't make him famous. At that time, his addiction was himself and every other addiction paled into insignificance. He built a rock-and-roll image because it looked good, but it wasn't working for him any more.'

Yet there was one agent who was prepared to take the risk: John Noel. Born into a working-class family in Manchester on Christmas Day 1952, John Noel Linnen was the son of a crane worker. By the age of twenty-five, he had set up a talent management agency under his name which was to 'embody both the dignity and pomp of the royal family, but also the creativity and edginess of punk rock'. Above all, John prided himself on being able to spot and bring on new talent.

His biggest break was signing Davina McCall for a lucrative two-year deal with Channel 4 in 1998. Two years later, she landed the job as the host of *Big Brother*, a hot new reality-TV show imported from Holland. When the winner of the first series, Craig Phillips, was inundated with media offers on his release from the house, Davina directed him to John, who was known as a tough operator who always sealed the best deals for his clients. It was a measure of John's clout that he pulled off a five-album record deal with WEA Records, worth a reported £500,000, on the back of it.

Since then, John had secured an iron grip on the *Big Brother* contestants, signing virtually every housemate with celebrity potential, from Nasty Nick to Jade Goody. He was to become indispensable not only to the show's production company, Endemol, but also to Channel 4 itself.

Though most agents would have run a mile, John's instinct was that Russell was talented enough to persevere with. Unlike other agents, he also knew from first-hand experience that heroin use didn't always have to mean the end of the line. Like Russell, Davina had had a fractured childhood, an eating disorder and a spell as an MTV presenter. Like Russell, she had also smoked heroin. Thanks to drug rehab, she had come out the other side, and was now the most successful female presenter on TV.

Davina recommended the person who had helped her beat her habit. Chip Somers was a former Radley public schoolboy who had become addicted to heroin in the sixties. For eighteen years, he struggled with his addiction, even going to prison for thirteen months for aggravated burglary. Despite overdosing several times, he finally realized he had to clean up when he took the money he was meant to use to buy food for his daughter and spent it on drugs instead. After coming clean, Chip had worked at rehab clinics Clouds and the Priory. It was there that Davina had met him. As she later recalled in an interview with *Bury Free Press*: 'I was in a meeting and I did not know anybody. It was one of those situations where you say to yourself that unless someone comes to speak to you in thirty seconds, you'll leave. Then Chip came up and shook my hand

and said "Are you new?" He then said, "Let me introduce you to some good girls," and that was it. I stayed. That is what Chip is good at. He helped me and will always be a very special person. I got myself clean after that by going to meetings.'

For the previous few years, Chip had been running his own drug treatment centre by the name of Focus 12 in Bury St Edmunds, Suffolk. As an enthusiastic champion and patron, Davina had just donated the £16,000 she won on *Celebrity Who Wants to Be a Millionaire?* to help Chip open its new premises in a Georgian townhouse close to the town centre.

When Russell was once again caught smoking heroin in the toilets, this time at his manager John Noel's Christmas party at the end of 2002, it was the final straw. Russell had rocked up with a homeless man by the name of Harmonica Matt. A trembling, shambolic wreck of a man, he was one of the strays that Russell had picked up along the way. The evening started badly when Harmonica Matt proceeded to leer at the female guests, in particular Davina McCall and Tess Daly. Russell retreated to the toilets, where he was discovered taking his fix. As he later revealed: 'They knew I took drugs, but they didn't know what drugs or how often. I wasn't very discreet.'

Now that John had caught Russell red-handed, he told him in no uncertain terms to get help, or forget about having any kind of career. Noting his embarrassingly fleeting appearance in *Cruise of the Gods* and the fact that he had not had a decent job offer in months, Russell finally got the message and agreed to be assessed.

'John took a rather dictatorial attitude to my drug use,' Russell recalled. 'Even when he was told, "There's no point trying to get anyone in treatment unless they want it," he said, "He's going." And that was it. Without that, I would have died.' A friend at the time added: 'His agent practically frogmarched Russell. He had no choice. John even offered to pay for it.'

On a freezing December day in 2002, Russell walked through the green front door of number 82 Risbygate Street, Bury St Edmunds. After a thorough assessment, Chip delivered his diagnosis. If Russell didn't stop taking drugs now, he would be dead, in a mental asylum or in jail within six months. Yet even after everything that had happened to him, a bit of Russell still aspired to self-destruct. He was shocked, but he later admitted to *The Observer* that part of him, when he heard the news, thought: 'Yeah, that's cool, man.'

As a condition of entering the three-month day-release programme, the first thing Russell was told to do was turn out his pockets and hand over any drugs he still had on him. As he braced himself, he was prescribed a powerful drug called Subutex. It was a 'short sharp shock' treatment to lesson the agonizing symptoms of going cold turkey, and help Russell's brain adjust to the withdrawal. What followed was the hardest forty-eight hours of Russell's life. As he sweated out the remains of toxins in his system, he suffered excruciating abdominal cramps, vomiting, runny eyes and severe headaches. When he came through the other side, Russell said he felt 'like a broken machine'.

Harrowing though the detox had been, clearing out his mind was to prove even more difficult. It was the start of an intense period of self-analysis for Russell, who was forced to probe back into his childhood for the reasons for his pain, which he had sought to dull with opiates. Some of the toughest parts of his rehabilitation were the emotional heart-to-hearts with his mum, Babs. He had always hated seeing his mother in tears. As Russell later admitted, he also 'did a lot of looking out of windows, crying'.

For a short time, the bulimia he had suffered from as a young teenager also returned. Following traumatic counselling sessions, sleeping pills were the only way he could escape the long wakeful nights rehashing past misdemeanours in his head. Stripped bare of excuses, he was forced to confront the truth – that he had lost all his jobs and Amanda, the love of his life, because he had been 'an unbearable arsehole'.

Chip's task was also to change Russell's mindset. Russell had taken drugs of some kind every day from the age of sixteen to the age of twenty-seven. They had become his reason for being and the first thing he thought about when he got up in the morning. Heroin had been his duvet, his security blanket, a comforting shield to fend off the world. Now Russell had to find other things to take their place, and accept that if he so much as touched another drug, his life was over.

The fact that he had opted to stay in a bed and breakfast, rather than join the residential rehab programme, demanded every ounce of his self-control. Yet Russell's strength of character meant it did not take long for him to find his resolve. When he was allowed on a Christmas exeat from rehab, he found himself chopping up coke for his friends, who urged him to have just one cheeky little line for old times' sake. He resisted. Giving up drugs filled him with mixed emotions. On one hand, they had been a central part of his life. He compared the feeling to 'losing a family member or losing access to an enthralling computer game you were really enjoying'. But on the other hand, Russell was euphoric to discover that he had the will to kick his habits.

An important aspect of the treatment was to restore the addict's confidence. For light relief, Russell had to engage in 'fun activities' to rebuild self-worth. Exercises on the programme included having a go at being the town crier for a day. There were also camping trips, visits to adventure playgrounds and go-kart circuits – even paper-dart-throwing competitions. As well as keeping a daily diary charting his changing emotions, Russell was encouraged to have a go at expressing his feelings through art, and to display his creations in the art therapy room.

Although Russell was winning his battle against narcotics and alcohol, there was one addiction he did not seem in a rush to beat. In his first week at Focus 12, he had been diagnosed as a sex addict. As a regular user of prostitutes, his behaviour had been described as 'compulsive and dangerous'.

While he was not allowed drugs, there was nothing to stop Russell chatting up and bedding women in the town. He found it gave him the same escape he got from booze and heroin. As he later wrote in *Elle* magazine: 'Deprived of narcotics in wildest Bury St Edmunds, my predatory nature and promiscuity had become ever more apparent. I hounded the market town's shop girls and waitresses with insatiable lust and a fortunate degree of metropolitan aplomb, which meant my desperate endeavours weren't entirely fruitless.'

When he had entered rehab, Russell had told few people where he was going. Now he had to shake off his old lifestyle – and even his old mates. 'He suddenly went off the radar, I couldn't get hold of him,' his friend Will Knott remembers. 'I rang up Matt and I said: "Look, Russ isn't returning my texts or calls. I rang him to say 'Happy Christmas' and he didn't answer the phone and he never sent anything back." Matt told me he had gone into rehab, and then after that, as I understand it, he wasn't really allowed to speak to me any more because I was so involved in the past two years of craziness. He was told he had to cut his ties with the past.'

CHAPTER NINE

RUSSELL REBORN

'It was as if Russell didn't know which path would turn out for him – comedian, actor, presenter or writer. He was betting on every horse and seeing which one would come home first.'

— ACTRESS WENDY DANVERS,
ON RUSSELL IN 2003

It was a very different Russell who walked out of number 82 Risbygate Street in the March of 2003. Feeling bruised from his experiences, and unsure of what to do next, he was like a lost soul.

'For the first six months or a year, it was like talking to a zombie. Russell was just really dead behind the eyes,' recalled fellow comedian Matt Blaize. 'Even when Russell was on drugs, he had this life and energy about him. Coming out [of rehab], he was bereft of all energy and expression. He had been an alcoholic from sixteen to twenty-six, smoking grass at fifteen, doing coke at seventeen and then heroin and crack for five years, so he was really fucked up by the detoxing. Really, it took him a couple of years to find his spirit and his energy levels again.'

Twice a week, Russell went back to Focus 12 for outpatient sessions. He also attended Narcotics, Alcoholics and Sex Addicts Anonymous meetings. As the old adage went, he took it one day at a time. Much as he yearned for a drink, a joint or even a puff of a cigarette to help him turn off his mind, Russell would religiously count the days since he took his last intoxicant. All the time he stayed clean, he never stopped missing the comfort drugs gave him when life got difficult.

With the help of more therapy, Russell was finally able to review his life with clarity. As part of the recovery process, he grieved not only for the child he had been, but also for the lost boy he had turned into. For hours, he watched replays of his old performances on MTV and *Re:Brand*, including his humiliating May Day protest. 'You could see my poor little hunted eyes,' he said later. 'I was just a silly boy who needed a big cuddle.'

Focus 12 was not Russell's only stint at a treatment centre. His management also paid for him to go to a facility in the US for therapy. Russell loathed the experience. The course involved long group sessions, in which Russell was meant to explore the deep-seated reasons behind his addictions. But Russell missed home and struggled to take it seriously. His counsellors constantly complained that instead of opening up to them, he would crack jokes.

Eventually, in a bid to get him to dig deep into his psyche, they encouraged him to take part in an anger exercise. After days of holding back, Russell worked himself into such a frenzy about his childhood that he picked up the chair he'd been sitting on and smashed it against a wall. Suddenly, he found himself at the centre of a security alert, during which he was restrained by the very counsellors who had tried to persuade him to unleash his fury in the first place.

The next thing he knew, he claimed he was taken to a nearby hospital's psychiatric unit to be independently assessed. It was a scene which Russell later described as being like something out of *One Flew Over the Cuckoo's Nest*. Just as he feared he would be incarcerated in a mental facility for the rest of his days, he was relieved to find that as soon as he said he was not medically insured, the authorities were apparently only too happy to send him on his way.

Russell was currently on a quest to find something that would fill the void left by drugs and alcohol. Therapy had taught him to evaluate his strengths and the importance of being healthy in order to get his life back in balance. His previous diet had consisted mainly of junk food. Now, he was most often to be found sipping green tea, and snacking on nuts and fruit.

Before rehab, the only form of physical exercise he had taken was, in his own words, 'fucking'. After, he took up kick-boxing and also Ashtanga, a particularly energetic style of yoga. Thanks to the location of his new flat, which his agent John Noel had helped him find (according to Russell, Noel also paid the rent for the next two years), Russell could practise his new hobby up to five times a week at trendy Triyoga in Primrose Hill, where he became a regular.

'He found he was very good at it,' observed a classmate. 'He could do all the most difficult poses. He stood at the front of the class and was chatty with the teachers.'

It was at one of these sessions that he bumped into *Little Britain*'s David Walliams, who was also a yoga devotee. The last time David had seen Russell was as he sailed off into the sunset leaving Russell behind, after Russell was sacked from *Cruise of the Gods*. Now, David saw him looking toned and glowing with health. He couldn't believe the change in Russell, and the pair were to become close friends.

For his own sake, Russell knew he had to keep busy. He hated sitting at home on the dole, eating Weetabix and watching daytime television. In his unemployed state, a programme on a cable channel called *Dogs with Jobs* plunged him into even deeper depression.

However, with time on his hands, Russell could read more deeply. As a younger man, Russell had skirted round subjects, reading beginner's guides on areas in which he was interested. He now learned about Eastern philosophy and became fascinated by the ideas of Arthur Schopenhauer, a nineteenth-century philosopher. Schopenhauer's teachings, which owe a lot to Buddhist thought, helped Russell form a new view of the world. He started seeing life in terms of energy and nature, taking long walks so he could feel closer to the elements.

To fill the hole left by drugs, Russell turned to religion. He had first come into contact with the Hare Krishna movement when he had toyed with making a programme about them for *Re:Brand*. He had asked to do some filming at one of their temples and been introduced to a devotee by the name of Vershana. 'When Russell came out of rehab, I got a call from him,' she recalls. 'He told me that he had been on drugs, but had now cleaned up his act, and he had some questions.'

After that, they regularly met at the Hare Krishna vegetarian restaurant, Govinda's, in Soho Street. During their meals, Russell wanted to know about the group's beliefs in karma and reincarnation. He also started visiting Bhaktivedanta Manor, the stately home near Watford, which had been donated to the movement by George Harrison in the early seventies. Russell attended the thirtieth anniversary celebrations. Although he had some doubts, he often returned when he had a free afternoon to talk to the Swamis, their spiritual leaders, about the religion.

On one occasion, he met a visiting guru called Radhanath Swami. Russell was struck by the holy man's tranquil calm and was thrilled to be told he could see the holiness within Russell. Encouraged, Russell went on to ask if he could be of service as a devotee, which would have meant shaving his head. But Russell was informed that he would be of more use spreading the word through his position in the media.

Therefore, as a simple follower, Russell was not expected to wear orange robes or shave his head. However, he would attend wearing prayer beads. He found that chanting helped him calm his nerves, especially before stand-up gigs. Vershana said: 'Sometimes Russell came on his own. Sometimes he came with friends. He was not your stereotypical Hare Krishna devotee, but Russell felt there were some aspects he could apply to his life. We would talk about what it was like to be a Hare Krishna and I found him to be a genuinely honest and upfront person. He did not try to hide anything about himself.'

According to Hare Krishna follower Radha Mohan, who also met Russell at the Manor: 'Russell is like many people who get into difficulties when they feel that this world is not everything that it should be. It takes a certain person to come to the Hare Krishna movement, someone who is open-minded, interested in philosophy and culture, and who reads a lot. It's for people who want answers. When Russell came out of rehab and went to the temple, it helped him a lot. I think he feels indebted. He was very receptive. I would compare his participation to George Harrison's, who was also a member, but never changed his appearance.'

With every day, Russell was feeling stronger. Painfully aware of the damage caused to his career, he knew it would take a great deal of work to rebuild his shattered reputation. He realized it was up to him to make opportunities for himself.

For years, he had believed he needed drugs to be creative. Now he had to prove to himself that that was not the case. He made several short films and even wrote a play – about a man who writes a play to get the girl he is in love with. He had some interest, and started sending out scripts to actors he thought would be right for the parts. One of the recipients was his old friend, veteran actress Wendy Danvers, whom he would sometimes ring for a chat.

Wendy recalled: 'Russell sent the script and addressed it to The Sexiest Woman in Weybridge, which must have made the postman jump a bit! At the time, it was as if he didn't know which path would turn out for him – comedian, actor, presenter or writer. He was betting on every horse and seeing which one would come home first.'

Within a month of Russell leaving rehab, John Noel had shown his faith in his protégé by becoming secretary of Vanity Projects, the dormant production company Russell had formed while he was at MTV. He reassured Russell that the work would soon be rolling in, and set about spreading the word about Russell's talents. In the meantime, Russell recorded some voice-over samples in the hope of getting some work on commercials or documentaries.

Yet stand-up remained Russell's first love – and he was determined to try again. Before rehab, he had depended on shock tactics. Now he knew he owed it to the audience to entertain them, too. Apart from anything else, he also needed to make a living, and stand-up was the only way he knew how. By the end of May 2003, he was back on stage at the Casablanca Club in London's West End, and was soon organizing twice-weekly comedy clubs with his close friend, comedian Paul Foot.

He still relied on some of his old comedy themes from the past, but now his routines were becoming more structured and better rehearsed. To mark the one-year anniversary of getting clean, in December 2003 he hosted a comedy show at the Enterprise in Camden, in support of Focus 12.

Thanks to his clout at Channel 4, John Noel was well placed to put Russell in pole position for any new job opportunities. 'Russell was a spent force and no one would touch him,' recalls a friend. 'It was harder for John to resurrect his career than if Russell had come from nothing, because he had burned so many bridges.'

Another TV insider observed: 'John Noel has been very instrumental in making Russell a success. He was pretty important in helping him through some of this. You have got to give him credit. I think he is therefore not possessive, but he clearly regards Russell as more than just an artist he represents.'

Russell's post-rehab breakthrough came when he was picked to be the latest young comedian to show off his talents on *Comedy Lab* for Channel 4. The pilot series was a great showcase for new and experimental comedy, and had helped launch the careers of Peter Kay and Dom Joly. The half-hour slot gave Russell a blank slate for whatever comedy ideas he felt like expressing.

As soon as the show was commissioned for broadcast in autumn 2003, the first person Russell got on board was his long-term friend Matt Morgan from his MTV and *Re:Brand* days. The programme was a joint production between Russell's Vanity Projects and So Television, the production company owned by Graham Norton. Every day, Russell would cycle down from north London to So's Waterloo offices.

Matt was to collaborate with Russell on the content. Thrilled to be reunited with each other on a project once again, they were soon back to their old ways, spending lunchtimes hanging out at a nearby language school in the hope of pulling some pretty foreign girls in need of a few extra-curricular English lessons.

The piece revisited many of Russell's favourite themes. The decapitated pig's head made another appearance as a member of the show's resident band, the Meat Beats. Russell's Elephant Man character also had a cameo, as did two dead mice, who appeared in between sketches as armchair critics.

Psychologists might have taken an interest in one particularly disturbing sketch, in which Russell looked back at his childhood through his 'retrospeculars'. Russell portrays himself as a simpering effeminate child, who begs his father to protect him from a hideous pink-Y-front-wearing imp doing a jig in the back garden. Despite his son's obvious terror, the uncaring father insists he has got to work, and shouts at Russell to go outside and play anyway. When Russell once again comes back to tell him what he has seen, his dad turns round to look at him – and has now changed into the monster Russell has been warning him about.

It was a mixed bag, and the links between the skits were sometimes awkward and forced. However, with the presenter dressed in a long black dress coat and a top hat, it was the first outing of Russell as a gothic master of ceremonies. His hair at the time was in a girlish sleek brown bob. But looking back now, there is something distinctly recognizable about the way Russell had backcombed and gelled the hair at the rear, so it stood up like a bird's nest. Inexplicably, the show signed off with Russell singing 'Karma Chameleon' as he grappled with a lady wrestler.

The only national paper review came, naturally, from Dominik Diamond in the *Daily Star*, who was also the sole TV reviewer to note Russell's recent absence from TV screens. He described the programme as: 'ostensibly a stage show in which Russell opined about freaks and misfits, it spun off into bizarre features and included a house band consisting of a dead pig and a hand. But it worked in a wonderful "early Vic Reeves" kind of way. I am amazed Brand hasn't become a huge star. Hopefully, this time he will be.'

CHAPTER TEN

BIG SUCCESS

'I was ill and this is
my redemption song.'

— RUSSELL ON HIS STAND-UP SHOW
BETTER NOW, 2004

Costume drama: as Russell starts to experiment with his image in the summer of 2005, there was more than a hint of his inner dandy in this period costume worn to an early eviction in *Big Brother 6*.

Quick, call Trinny and Susannah!: A week later, Russell turned up to the filming in a grey suit and flip-flops.

Eroticised Humour, Edinburgh Fringe, August 2005: Russell's last stand-up show before his dramatic image change.

First steps in a new direction: two months after the end of *Big Brother 6*, Russell is now moving towards a more gothic look.

New year, new tight trousers: with Davina McCall on *Celebrity Big Brother*, in January 2006.

Kate in the act, 24 May 2006: Russell makes a run for it after being caught by the paparazzi the morning after spending the night at Kate Moss's house in St John's Wood. It became the tabloid image of the summer and sealed Russell's reputation as Britain's most famous philanderer.

The secret's out: Kate left by the front door as Russell sprinted over a rear wall. Desperate to keep the relationship under wraps, she was exasperated to be caught out.

Russell and Rod's daughter: the pair hit it off when they met in June 2006; here Kimberly Stewart enters Russell's flat in the early hours of the morning (*left*).

Stand-off: Rod and Russell smooth things over, moments after the rocker forced Russell to deny publicly he ever slept with his daughter, at the *GQ* Men of the Year awards in September 2006.

Another conquest: Cassie Sumner had a
serious relationship with Russell, which
ended in January 2006. Her story appeared
in *The People* newspaper six months later.

Russell performs *Shame*, his third sell-out show
at the Edinburgh Fringe, August 2006.

Proud mother: Russell's mum Babs loyally attends every important event in her son's life. Here she turns out to support him the night he filmed his live comedy DVD at the Shepherd's Bush Empire in October 2006.

Avid fan: by autumn 2006, Russell was such a recognizable figure that he was spawning imitators – Avid Merrion pulled off this hysterical parody of Russell in October.

Showbiz royalty at last: Russell films a skit with rocker Courtney Love for the eponymous *Russell Brand Show* in November 2006.

As Russell proves once again in *Little Britain Live*, in aid of Comic Relief, there is nothing he won't do in the name of comedy.

Finally, after weeks of negotiation, the deal for the show that was to revive Russell Brand's career was signed and sealed. But this was no ordinary contract. There were clauses and sub-clauses hammered out after long meetings with lawyers.

Russell had had to attend numerous auditions even to get this far. To each he had turned up on time, immaculately dressed, and given a professional and focused performance. Furthermore, he faithfully promised he would continue to attend NA and AA meetings, and even that he would not sleep with anyone working on the programme.

Most of the clauses amounted to get-outs so that, in the event that Russell relapsed or misbehaved, he could be fired at a moment's notice. It was a risk, but one that Channel 4 was willing to take. It was the fifth series of *Big Brother*, May 2004, and makers Endemol needed something fresh and exciting. The novelty of the show was wearing thin, leading to falling ratings and poor reviews.

In an effort to revive the format, the airtime of the main *Big Brother* show was to be doubled. Plus, three times a week, new spin-off programme *Efourum* would feature critics, fans and celebs, as well as friends and relatives of the housemates, who would answer questions from a studio audience. In turn, they would also give their opinions on the goings-on inside the *BB* house.

Getting the right host to bring together all the elements of the show was crucial, and it was felt that Russell fitted the profile. He was young, good-looking and edgy, while his appearances on the MTV phone-in show *Select* had shown his warmth and humour with the public, and also that he was capable of juggling the demands of live TV.

For his part, Russell had barely even seen *Big Brother*. But he was determined to repay Channel 4's trust in him. Deep down, he still harboured fears that he might lose everything again in one ill-judged 'fuck-it-I'll-do-it-anyway' moment. For all the ladders he was climbing, Russell knew one slip-up would send him sliding back down that snake. And this time, the game would be over.

As an ever present reminder to himself to behave, he kept a framed copy of his 'UB40' (as he called his P45 tax form) on his shelf, to make him think about what it had felt like to be unemployed in the days after he came out of rehab. As he later recalled to the *Evening Standard*: 'There was a real fear that I'd walk on and go, "Fuck off, you cunts, Ian Huntley is brilliant." I just thought I'd tourettically shout something that you can't take back. I always wanted to be successful and the first time I had it, I fucked it up.'

The first show was broadcast on 31 May 2004, in front of a studio audience of forty. Seated behind a giant fluorescent lilac desk, Russell swivelled on his chair and waved his hands around expansively, as he was prone to do when he was nervous. His loose brown curls hung casually around his face and he wore a khaki army jacket over a pink T-shirt, as he attempted to drum up enthusiasm about the new *Big Brother* series.

His efforts were thrown slightly off-course when celebrity guest Nancy Sorrell said that she had given up watching *Big Brother* and that putting the new housemates together in one room was a cynical attempt to get them to have sex on screen. Quickly, Russell used his humour as his ringmaster's whip, retorting: 'The show has only just begun. I've got to be the Dimbleby figure here. Calm yourself, girl!'

It was a strong start. *Efourum* was a verbal free-for-all, which could easily have descended into chaos had it not been for Russell's control. He would jokingly scold audience members who argued with one another, and cut people off if necessary, but with charm. He played the cheeky cockney rascal to the hilt, occasionally using a verbal flourish. Overall, he had the geniality and intelligence to make the most pedestrian audience comments come alive as comic moments.

Beneath the apparent anarchy, Russell was consumed by getting his performance right. He would comb replays of the show for mistakes, looking for tips on how he could improve. As very much an experimental offshoot of the main show, audience figures were modest. Those critics who did comment on the programme, however, felt that Russell had got the tone exactly right by not taking himself or *Big Brother* too seriously. It was no surprise when the first thumbs-up came from the ever loyal *Daily Star* TV critic Dominik Diamond, who cooed: 'Haven't I told you how brilliant Russell Brand is? For years now? Have you seen him on *Big Brother's Efourum*? It's beautiful being this right.' When the series reached the end of its two-and-a-half-month run, Russell was proud that he had not let so much as a swear word slip. It felt like a major achievement that the job had not ended with a scene or a sacking.

Although Russell's TV career was flourishing, he was nevertheless determined to make a success of his stand-up. Following his shameful departure from the Edinburgh Fringe two years earlier, Russell was nervous about his return and anxious to atone for his bad behaviour. His last visit, by his own admission, had been a disgrace. In preparation for his comeback, he meticulously rehearsed his new act at small pubs and clubs all over London and the Midlands. Entitled *Better Now*, it was billed as 'shockingly honest tales of whores, heroin and hairdos'.

The piece was different from anything that Russell had done before. In 1980, American comic genius Richard Pryor had set himself on fire while freebasing cocaine. He was horribly burned, but turned his drugs experiences into a legendary stand-up show, *Live on the Sunset Strip*. Poignant yet funny, his tales of degradation were totally without self-pity. For one gag, Pryor waved a lit match and asked the audience to guess what it was. The punchline was that it was him, running down the street. For Russell, it was an inspiration.

'The thing about heroin is that it's very moreish' was Russell's arresting opening line. From there, the routine chronicled his descent into sex, sleaze and madness during his MTV and *Re:Brand* days. To illustrate exactly how low he had sunk, Russell arranged for a giant TV screen to replay the humiliating footage of his antics at the May Day riot. He summed up the whole show to the *Sunday Mail* with the words: 'It is biographical and embarrassing. I've changed. I'm clean, sober and the show is good.'

It was also clear that Russell was desperate to make amends. His interviews to publicize *Better Now* were like a mea culpa to everyone who had known him at his worst. 'I'm ashamed I was not nice to people,' he admitted later. 'I haven't made it up to everyone because there are a lot of people. It would be like Saddam Hussein making it up to individual Kurds by going round with a box of Quality Street.'

In place of the boorish loudmouth, there was a new, humbler – even spiritual – Russell. He was deeply apologetic and demure. 'I've learned that grand principles and ideas are meaningless if in your daily behaviour you are an arsehole,' he told *Time Out*'s Malcolm Hay. He also said to the Edinburgh Fringe newspaper, *Fest*: 'I know, particularly in comedy circles, I've got a bad reputation because I have behaved really badly for a long while. But I was ill and this is my redemption song.

'I am genuinely trying to make the world better. I think

that shows and it doesn't matter what people think of you. If inside yourself you just want to do good, then you'll be okay. But it's a hard course to steer because I think my internal moral compass does point towards hell.' He added to interviewer Dorian Nicholas: 'I try to be truthful now and I have ideals and intentions beyond the remit of just making loads of money and being famous.'

After the opening night on the Fringe at The Pleasance, critics agreed that the show's title, *Better Now*, was not only a fair description of Russell's state of health, but also his comedy. Bruce Dessau said that, unlike his previous ramblings, Russell's anecdotes were now 'precision tuned'. Festival magazine *Three Weeks* raved: 'By the end of the show, every woman was in love with him.' Meanwhile, *The Guardian* weighed in, saying that come the finale of the set, 'You'd rather hug him than hit him', adding that it was 'an accomplished comeback'. Even *The Times* called the act 'a bit of a belter'. *Metro* summed it up with the words: 'A few years ago, his wide-boy geezer banter was only good for offending punters. He's definitely better now and he has a hit on his hands.'

Those who had known Russell in his old life were stunned by the transformation. Matt Blaize said: 'Before, Russell was so pained and tortured that the last thing he probably really wanted to do was be funny. While he was in rehab, the penny dropped with him. That year, 2004, was the first time I had ever seen Russell write jokes in a structured way. *Better Now* was a great performance. It could have been really self-indulgent – but he walked that line between self-analysis and self-deprecation beautifully. It was poignant and well judged.' The production was a triumph. Russell left Edinburgh with renewed confidence, and even talked about taking the show to America.

Now that he didn't drink, Russell's biggest challenge was knowing what to do with himself after gigs. Before he went on stage, he would do yoga and chant the Hare Krishna mantra.

But he found it impossible to face the adrenalin comedown alone.

He confessed to one interviewer he wouldn't even consider a gig a performance without the sex afterwards. As he was later to tell Piers Morgan: 'You have all this velocity and then nothing. And I just come off stage thinking: "Fuck it. I have got to have a hit or a fuck – or something, anything, just to keep this buzz going. I can't let this energy just peter out into the darkness of the night, or just lie in bed and do nothing."'

In the past, Russell had gone to Sex Addicts Anonymous meetings, but didn't identify with the types he saw attending sessions in 'a church basement crawling with mildew'. In his own mind, he wasn't really convinced he was doing anything wrong anyway. Russell argued that sex was the most natural thing in the world. If it wasn't, he reasoned, the human race wouldn't exist.

Almost two years after he entered rehab, he claimed to have weaned himself off prostitutes, but otherwise admitted he was not too fussy about who he slept with. 'The problem is that unless I am careful, I will try to seduce any woman at any time regardless of cost or consequence,' he wrote in *Elle*. 'There are no other factors because it's not about them – it's about me. Many women and men speak of having a type: "I like black women" or "I crave fellas with thin legs". My sole criteria is "Will she sleep with me?"'

Just as he had with drugs, Russell needed sex to turn off his brain: 'It's about escape – a few hours of being out of my head.' It was a way to 'get high – to anaesthetize the ever nagging mind'. Not sounding entirely convinced, Russell added: 'I try – I try – to behave with control and dignity around women. It's harder than giving up smack.'

Although Russell had promised not to sleep with anyone working on *Big Brother*, there was apparently no clause stopping him from bedding former housemates. And the sleazier their behaviour in front of the cameras, the more Russell seemed to like them.

As a late arrival to the *Big Brother* house in 2004, Becki Seddiki was sent in to shake up the status quo. Once inside, the former lap dancer's claim to fame was her swift announcement of her bisexuality and the removal of her top to show off her surgically enhanced 34DD breasts. She found herself voted off after twelve days, to be greeted by the news that her Muslim family was so ashamed they had disowned her.

Becki had met Russell when she was invited on to *Efourum*. As she was to tell the *Sunday Mirror* eighteen months later, she was walking down Camden High Street when a black people carrier taxi pulled up alongside her. 'Suddenly, I heard a shout: "Oi! All right, darlin'? Blimey, you look like a bit of all right. I've been checking out your arse, you've got that special wiggle, it really turns me on."' Assuming Russell knew her, Becki got in the car. She later discovered he hadn't recognized her at all. However, she found Russell too good-looking to resist and the next night ended up at his flat, drinking wine while Russell quoted French existentialist philosopher Jean-Paul Sartre.

Nevertheless, their liaison was to be short-lived. In between their meetings, she said Russell would bombard her with flirty and highly suggestive texts, as well as suggestions for adventurous sex. Yet when they did meet, any bedroom activity was perfunctory. Becki went on to relate how, several weeks later, she was dismayed to see Russell walk into a party with 'a girl who looked like a model'. 'I was really upset,' she said. 'I couldn't believe he hadn't had the decency to tell me he had moved on. At some point, he came over and chatted to me – when his girlfriend had gone to the loo, I presume. I was polite, but it was a bit frosty. After that, he invited me to some of his gigs and TV shows, but I couldn't make it.'

Meanwhile, the TV opportunities were flooding in. Channel 4 was actively looking for new vehicles for him. There was talk of his own show, provisionally called *The Crazy World of Russell Brand*, created by the same team behind *Banzai*. The concept was to collect 'some of the craziest people from around the world and some of Britain's hottest young comedians for one mad night'. In addition, it was a measure of how much Russell had repaired his reputation that he was also being considered as the new face of the channel's breakfast TV programme. A half-hour pilot of *The Good, The Bad and the Early*, a live topical debate show fronted by Russell, was filmed. He didn't land the job, but it demonstrated that Russell had regained the trust of the people who mattered.

Russell rounded off the year with an appearance in a one-off Christmas special called *A Bear's Christmas Tail*. It was a spin-off of *Bo! Selecta,* featuring Russell's agency stablemate Leigh Francis as a foul-mouthed teddy bear. With their manager John Noel as executive producer, it was also a showcase for the artists on his books, including Davina McCall, Kirsty Gallacher, Craig Phillips and Dermot O'Leary. Russell played a deranged wolf and a ringmaster. They were the sort of surreal offbeat acting roles that suited him best.

When a celebrity version of *Big Brother* aired in January 2005, featuring Caprice, racing pundit John McCririck and former Happy Mondays dancer Bez, it was felt that *Efourum* had worked so well that it deserved to go up to five days a week.

Now that he was in regular employment, Russell was in a position to buy his own home. During his search, in typical fashion, Russell had used his charm to seduce one of the estate agents in the bedroom of a property they were viewing together.

Finally, on 18 May 2005, Russell took possession of his first flat. He paid £280,000 for the one-bedroom bachelor pad on the ground floor of a Victorian house. The setting was a quiet tree-lined street in Gospel Oak, between Kentish Town and Hampstead. The area suited Russell because it was not far from his agent John Noel's office in Chalk Farm, nor his favourite hang-outs in Camden. He also loved the fact it was just a five-minute walk to Hampstead Heath.

The place was perfect. It had a small, enclosed patio at the back and stripped wooden floors throughout. Russell had a cat flap fitted in the front door for his black-and-white tomcat, Morrissey. Underneath the doorbell, he simply wrote 'Russell' in biro. The new homeowner enjoyed decking out his property with Habitat-style furniture and scented candles.

That same month, *Efourum* was reborn as *Big Brother's Big Mouth*. As the jewel in its ratings crown, Channel 4 was desperate to expand the franchise still further. Screened on Channel 4 at 7.30 p.m., it was Russell's first foray into prime time.

No longer tied to sitting behind a desk, Russell could get out there among the audience. There were new ideas, including 'Textual Preference', where the public was polled on a range of topics associated with the housemates. There was also '*Big Brother*'s Mouthpiece', a 24-hour telephone-answering service people used to vent their spleen about the goings-on.

Slowly, Russell's confidence and sense of the ridiculous were starting to return. The father of one contestant, Craig, initially refused to shake his hand because he thought Russell had been too cruel about his son. Russell became so obsessed with custard that the show's producer warned him they would make him present the programme from a wheelie bin full of the stuff if he didn't stop going on about it.

As ever, Russell thrived on the excitement of live television. He told journalist Benjie Goodhart: 'I find it exhilarating. I really like live television. I think you get an authenticity you simply can't recreate in an edit. And I think people are more tolerant if something does seem to be a bit chaotic. I like it being live. I embrace it. We had Kitten just walk off the show last year. It was brilliant.

'What frightens me isn't live TV, it's going into a shop and ordering a loaf of bread. That's when I think, "Oh God, the mundanity of it all. We are all going to die. Death is approaching. There is no poetry in this moment." But when things are a bit chaotic, I get excited.'

In interviews, it was clear that Russell was getting back into his stride, standing up for the series and emphasizing its worth. 'Ultimately, I am just talking about human nature. I've got quite a lot of freedom and I am just dealing with people. *Big Mouth* is an incredibly egalitarian show. The audience have got equal billing with the guests and I think I appear lower down the bill than them. They're a belligerent bellicose mob who are quite happy to bellow me into submission at the slightest provocation.'

His farewell of 'Hare Krishna' was soon becoming his trademark. It was, according to Radha Mohan, Russell's attempt to pass on the message of his beliefs subtly, without forcing it down viewers' throats. 'By saying "Hare Krishna" at the end of the programme, Russell is trying to spiritually elevate his audience and make them feel more peaceful and help them in their spiritual lives. He is doing something very noble and very pure. He marries his relationship with Krishna consciousness with his professional career. He keeps things simple when he works them into his media, but he is aware of the depths of the Eastern philosophy – he believes in reincarnation and the effect of saying "Hare Krishna".'

However, Russell's mind was on matters of a strictly non-spiritual nature when he met ejected *Big Brother* housemate Makosi. The former cardiac nurse was caught on camera during the show having sex in the swimming pool. 'I found Makosi incredibly attractive,' he said afterwards. 'I have a thing for women who are cruel and powerful the way she is.'

Backstage, Russell asked for her phone number and called her 'a dirty cow'. In an interview with *Closer* magazine, Makosi later disclosed how Russell started to assail her with eight texts a day. 'Most of them were fairly filthy, but they made me laugh. He had the ability to be naughty, but not offensive, and make you feel like you were the only girl in the world.'

Back at his flat, Russell's seduction techniques were ... unusual. 'He came into the bedroom wearing a pair of Y-fronts, fluffy socks and a pyjama top. Then he stripped off his pants and began strutting around the room, talking as if he was a theatrical nineteenth-century poser. He asked if I liked his winky.'

According to Makosi, their relationship faded when she was so embarrassed by the allegations in the *News of the World* that she was a high-class prostitute that she stopped returning his calls. But for his part, Russell hinted that he had already had enough anyway, commenting to *Cosmopolitan* after the affair ended: 'There's only so much Makosi you can take.'

Even with his TV career blossoming, Russell was committed to keeping his comedy going. As ever, he wanted to tackle the grander themes. So, in the summer of 2005, he returned to the Edinburgh Fringe with his show *Eroticised Humour,* in which he addressed two of his favourite subjects: sex and death. It was 'part two' of his journey through the underworld, in which he retold stories of how he had bought sex toys from gay shops for *Re:Brand,* and his unedifying experience at an orgy.

At this time, Russell was linked with yet another housemate by dating Kate Lawler of *Big Brother 3*. They met at the Edinburgh Festival, where she was also doing a show. Kate confirmed they were mates, but insisted to the *News of the World* that it was nothing more: 'We got on really well. We've been out a few times, but we're just mates. We haven't even snogged.'

Increasingly, critics were often surprised by the contrast between the erudite storyteller on stage and the yobby big mouth who had a day job as a *Big Brother* presenter. *The Scotsman* called Russell 'a brilliant, literate raconteur with a gloriously over-the-top way with words and an apparently insatiable appetite for all things sexual'. Dominic Maxwell of *The Times* felt the show was rough around the edges, but predicted that: 'If he can gather his thoughts to full effect, Brand will be capable of greatness.'

After *Big Brother 6* finished, Russell hosted *Kings of Comedy* for E4. The four-week series saw four rising comedians and four veterans compete in a reality-TV set-up. The winner was to star in their own TV special, which was meant to be their big break. The comedians had to perform to live audiences and then one comic was axed through a public vote. The highlights were shown on Channel 4.

The programme was a welcome opportunity for Russell to reminisce with Karen Koren of the Gilded Balloon, who was a judge on the series. She had not seen him since the disastrous night back in 2002 when he gashed his leg as he was forcibly removed from her venue.

The show didn't always go entirely smoothly. At one point, Russell evicted the wrong contestant. When he realized his mistake, he had to push the bemused comic back on stage while ushering out the actual loser. But as the *Daily Mirror* commented: 'Luckily for Russ, we were probably the only ones watching.'

Out of the line-up, it was Russell who was picked as the natural star. According to the *Liverpool Echo*: 'No offence to Mick Miller or Stan Boardman, both still going down well with the punters, but the funniest man has to be the surreal, manic, arm-waving presenter Russell Brand. Give that man his own stand-up show, or at least let him replace Davina McCall on *Big Brother* next year.'

CHAPTER ELEVEN

IMAGE IS EVERYTHING

*'The reason I look nice now is
because I like what I am.
There is a continuity between
the way I appear and the way
that I act. A bit Victorian, a
little bit camp and decadent in
a controlled fashion.'*

— RUSSELL IN *GQ* MAGAZINE,
OCTOBER 2006

Russell entered 2006 hopeful that this would be his year. With several interesting offers on the table, he was starting to feel that achieving his ambitions finally lay within reach. Yet not even he could have foreseen how quickly, or to what extent, they were shortly to be realized.

During one eviction show of *Big Brother 6* the previous summer, Russell had looked the best he had ever looked. His skin was buffed and tanned. A pale lemon shirt revealed the barest hint of a hairy chest, while his brown leather bomber jacket occasionally rode up to expose a flat, yoga-honed stomach. His whole image screamed smooth and expensively dressed TV presenter.

Though it was generally agreed that Russell had done an excellent job hosting the *Big Brother* offshoot, he was still very much a celebrity-in-waiting. While the more middle-of-the-road presenters Dermot O'Leary and Davina McCall were household names, Russell was, in the words of one reviewer, 'the unsung genius'. So unsung, in fact, that throughout the whole run of *Big Brother 6* he received only four passing mentions in the national press, and three of those were in the *Daily Star*.

For the last two years, Russell had been waiting for people to recognize him. Now, with an impending dramatic change of image, he was to give them no choice.

A chance meeting with Carl Barat of the Dirty Pretty Things set the ball rolling. They had first met the July before, when Russell had been invited to host a benefit at the

Camden Underworld. From Elvis to Michael Jackson, Russell had always loved stars who ooze glamour. He was particularly taken with the louche rock-star appearance of Carl, Pete Doherty's former partner in The Libertines.

Carl was dressed, in Russell's own words, like 'a troubadour assassin'. Instantly, Russell was smitten. Carl was everything Russell aspired to be, 'a quintessential Englishman: eccentric, romantic, charming and noble,' but with the cockney rasp of Harry H. Corbett. As a Libertine with Doherty, Carl had been obsessed with an idealized view of an England he called Albion, inspired by the poets Coleridge and Blake, where artful dodgers were as British as Dickensian dandies.

Both former drama students, Russell and Carl shared unhappy childhoods and cockney choirboy looks. Both had been through drugs, and were prone to depression. But with his wardrobe of trainers, sports shirts and jeans, by comparison with Carl, Russell felt boring and straight.

The turning point came a few weeks later, on 16 July 2005, when Russell hosted Carl's Dirty Pretty Things night at the Koko Club in Camden. To add to the atmosphere, Carl asked Russell to dress in a red jacket like a Victorian ringmaster. Exhibitionist though he was, Russell was apprehensive. But when Carl explained that it was to give the evening more of a traditional music-hall feel, Russell agreed. As a thank you, at the end of the night, Carl presented Russell with the antique silver-topped cane he had been carrying. It immediately became Russell's favourite prop. Together with Carl's skinny scarf, which he tied rakishly around his neck, the two accessories were to be the inspiration for Russell's new image.

It was a shameless rip-off of his friend's look, as Russell admitted on XFM: 'I prefer to spend time with musicians ... and then my own little personality collapsed like a meringue and I went and started dressing like Carl Barat. It's also like Johnny Cash and also Morrissey, who said he wore black on the outside because black was how he felt on the inside. But what pushed me over the edge was Carl Barat.'

Yet it demanded a delicate balance. While Russell aspired to evoke a Victorian dandy, the last thing he wanted to look like was an extra from a BBC costume drama. He consulted his old friend, stylist Sharon Smith, whom he had known since his MTV days, and together they set to work to create an image that suited Russell.

The presenter had always loved showing off his body in tight clothing, and it was agreed that torso-hugging shirts gave him a swashbuckling look. Mostly, they were left unbuttoned – according to Russell, in *The Guardian*, 'so people can see my body. They can have a look and see if they want to have sex with it. All my shirts are adapted to reveal nippers.'

Both he and Sharon felt that adopting the new trend for skinny jeans would give his style a sharper edge. Sharon would go one step further by seeking out testicle-crunching designs made for women.

Before, Russell's hair had been a glossy chestnut colour. He had first backcombed the back of his hair for his *Comedy Lab* appearance at the end of 2003, saying that it had given him 'a punk, post-modern look'. Now his locks were dyed black, left long and backcombed at the rear to offset his slightly oblong face and curb any resemblance to Christ. The secret, as he told *Loaded*, was 'commitment, back-combing and hairspray'.

To complete the gothic vampire look, the golden tan he had sported was allowed to fade, leaving his face and body a wan, pale colour, and his brown eyes were outlined with kohl. The revamp was finished with some manly stubble. Russell could be self-conscious about his toothy smile and he felt the bearded look detracted from it.

Consciously or unconsciously, Russell's new appearance also tapped into a trend known as EMO, short for 'emotionally hard core'. A breed of new goths, influenced by American bands like My Chemical Romance, EMO looks were based around dyed black hair, often wispy and trained over one eye, as well as lashings of black eyeliner. Devotees also wore mostly black and prided themselves on clever use of language. The trend had already been translated on to the catwalk with a fashion for skull scarves.

Back home in Essex, Russell's new image certainly got the net curtains twitching. Neighbours who previously remembered him rolling up to visit his mum Babs in jeans, T-shirt and white trainers were now taken aback to see him turning up in a cape. When questioned about Russell's bizarre get-up, his resolutely heterosexual dad Ron was at pains to stress that this was not the real Russell, and that he was really a jeans-and-trainers sort of boy at heart. 'He's still a quiet lad and the confident extrovert you see on TV is just a performance,' he told the *Daily Mirror*. 'He used to dress very normally until about a year ago when he got a stylist and now he wears all those strange clothes. It's just a phase he's going through. He looks like a star.'

At times, Russell seemed defensive about accusations that he had contrived his image. 'I didn't emerge from the womb with this ludicrous haircut wearing pointy boots, talking all Victorian,' he said in *The Independent on Sunday*. 'But neither did I sit plotting in an attic and thinking, "Ooh, it would be good if I suddenly spoke like that, if I mangled grammar a bit and started to wear tight clothes." These things are accumulative, like anybody's identity is accumulative.' He added in a *GQ* interview: 'The reason I look nice now is because I like what I am. There is a continuity between the way I appear and the way that I act. A bit Victorian, a little bit camp and decadent in a controlled fashion.'

Yet at other times, Russell seemed happy to make fun of himself. By his own admission, he now 'dressed like a twat'; he would later send up his dress sense as an odd sexual fetish practised behind closed doors in Essex. He also joked that he quickly learned not to be flattered if he was asked if he was in a band, because most of the time the questioner had mistaken him for Darkness singer Justin Hawkins.

Now all that was needed was for Russell to let his flowery language take flight. He had always enjoyed making the most of the comic juxtaposition between his impressive vocabulary and his 'Cor, blimey' accent. It had been a part of his stand-up in recent years, but now he decided to express it to the full. He peppered his language with words like 'thusly', 'quotidien' and 'swine'. Although the word most often used to describe his way of speaking was 'Dickensian', Russell had never read any Dickens, admitting somewhat sheepishly that the closest he had come was seeing *Blackadder's Christmas Carol* and *The Muppet Christmas Carol*.

Friends who had known Russell for years agreed that in fact his new look was not manufactured out of nowhere, but was rather a concentration of his mannerisms and interests dating back almost a decade. Ever since drama school, Russell had been fascinated by the darker side of Victoriana, whether it was Jack the Ripper, Oscar Wilde or John Merrick, the Elephant Man, who had become a curiosity in the 1880s.

'He has just exaggerated who he is,' says Matt Blaize, who first met Russell shortly after Drama Centre. 'He was like a throwback to an old Dickens novel when I first met him. He has just taken what he does best and packaged it. He has always dressed a bit cool and sexy. Now he camps it up and it has made him bigger.' Indeed, the clues were there all along. He had presented one episode of *Re:Brand* in a Victorian bowler, and *Comedy Lab* in a black frock coat and top hat.

Within the first week of *Celebrity Big Brother's Big Mouth* in January 2006, people were starting to sit up and take notice. *People* TV critic Gary Bushell was the first to be struck by Russell's unusual get-up: 'He may look like a trainee wizard, but he's smart, funny, down-to-earth and he loves TV ... the next Jonathan Ross?' Writing in the *Mirror*, *GMTV*'s Fiona Phillips had also spotted Russell. 'He's a complete one-off, refreshingly different, very warm and funny, a sort of latter-day Arthur Askey. He's going to be huge.' Victor Lewis-Smith in the *Evening Standard* mentioned Russell's new look, calling him a Jesus Christ lookalike, before adding unkindly that he was 'not merely at ease with his own stupidity, but positively revelling in it'.

Now that he finally had his confidence back after rehabilitation, Russell also wanted to revive some other aspirations. Long before he had become a comic, he had dreamed of being a film star. He had first fallen in love with the silver screen on his visits to the State cinema in Grays. When Russell had said, at the age of sixteen in the *Thurrock Gazette*, that he wanted to be a movie star, it had seemed a wild ambition. But now, he was acting in a Hollywood film called *Penelope*. It starred Reese Witherspoon, who was also the producer, as well as Christina Ricci in the title role. So far, most of Russell's dramatic parts had been criminals, drug dealers or rock stars – and this was no exception. Just as in his very first theatrical role, he was playing the part of nightclub owner Sam – without whom, Russell joked, 'the film would be a waste of an hour and a half.'

Described as a modern-day fable, *Penelope* is the whimsical tale of a rich girl (played by Ricci) who is cursed by having a nose like a pig's snout. As well as having a subtle subtext about tabloid intrusion, Witherspoon added: 'It has an uplifting message and a great story about learning to appreciate who you are.'

For Russell, it was a small step in the right direction. Ultimately, his aim was to have a career like his hero Richard Pryor's. He wanted to switch between making movies and huge rock-show-style stand-up gigs, performing to as many as

10,000 people. 'Television is not a long-term thing for me. I'll do it for a while because I enjoy it,' he told *The Telegraph* in June, just as his star was on the rise. 'I will do it for a while because I enjoy it and the money's good, but in the long run, I have a very clear idea of what I want.'

As ever, Russell's love life was colourful. While he claimed to have weaned himself off prostitutes, an assortment of models – several of them of the Page Three variety – came and went. Few of his relationships seemed to last very long.

In 2005, he had dated *Penthouse* cover girl Cassie Sumner, even going on holiday with her to the US. Cassie's 34DD debut in the *Daily Star* three years earlier had been captioned: 'Cassie Sumner is hoping to reach giddy heights as a glamour model. The twenty-year-old Kent cutie has got some pretty impressive foothills, and there are plenty of fellas who would be interested in tackling her upper slopes.'

That had set the tone for her career in newspapers, where she became a regular feature on the kiss-and-tell circuit. Starting with a tale about how Prince Harry had snogged her and run his fingers 'playfully up and down her thighs', she had gone on to clock up further stories on footballers Celestine Babayaro and Anthony Gardner, as well as *Emmerdale* actor Ben Freeman. Later, she would feature in two reports that she was a high-class escort girl: claims that she denied.

With his taste for busty women, Russell didn't seem to mind his girlfriend's questionable past, nor did he appear to worry that he was likely to be the subject of her next exposé in a national newspaper. It was a measure of how much his celebrity status was to change that Russell appeared very far down Cassie's PR agent's guest list for her birthday party at the Eve Club on 14 January 2006 – well behind several Z-list Page Three girls.

When Russell was offered a gig hosting the *NME* Awards for Channel 4 at the Hammersmith Palais in February, he was ecstatic. Two days earlier, he had been named *Time Out* Stand-Up Comedian of the Year. The contenders were chosen after consultation with comedy promoters. Considering that past winners of the comedy awards had included Harry Hill and Russell's idol Eddie Izzard – and bearing in mind that he had never won anything in his life before – it was his proudest achievement to date.

The *NME* event was an opportunity for another early outing of his new look. Wearing the most expensive item he had ever worn, a long frock coat costing £800 made by top designer Alexander McQueen, and accessorizing with a trendy skinny scarf, Russell looked more like a rock star than most of the nominees at the awards. The script for the ceremony, which contained some irreverent digs aimed at some of music's biggest names, was co-written with his mate Matt Morgan.

As it turned out, the evening was to require every bit of Russell's quick thinking and disaster management. If he really loved the chaos of live television, then this was to be his night.

Russell had already had a big laugh out of introducing a link from Bono saying he was appearing 'live from a satellite orbiting his own ego'. Now he was daring to take a pop at another rock star, 'Saint' Bob Geldof, as he presented the award for Best DVD. Russell began by cracking a gag about how sorry he was that his own choice, *Big Natural Tits 10*, had been pipped at the post by Geldof's *Live 8* DVD. As Geldof sloped up on to the stage with a face like thunder, Russell sensed there would be trouble when the singer shook his hand, but wouldn't look him in the eye. His instincts were proved right. Geldof crossed to the other side of the stage and hissed into the microphone: 'Russell Brand, what a cunt!'

Although not entirely unexpected, it was a kick in the teeth. What shocked Russell most was the fact that the c-word had been delivered by 'a man who's been canonized'. He was also upset because he knew his mum Babs was watching the show. As he later reflected: 'It was like being told to fuck off by Father Christmas.'

Now he was in a moral dilemma. Should he retaliate against a man considered a living saint for bringing the Ethiopian famine to the attention of the world? If he was in any doubt as to whether or not he should unleash the riposte, his mind was made up when he saw Matt standing in the wings, flashing him the thumbs-up. Once Geldof was back in his seat, Russell delivered the line with the ice-cold concentration of an assassin: 'No wonder Bob Geldof is such an expert on famine. He's been dining out on "I Don't Like Mondays" for thirty years.' It was clear from Russell's serious tone that this was more than just a punchline. There was no laughter from the audience, just gasps that Russell had dared to take on one of the nation's holy cows. As the camera panned to Geldof, there was little he could do but glare and accept that he had set himself up for it.

Virtually no press picked up on the remark, and if it had not been for the fact that Russell had mentioned it in interviews and made it a subject for his stand-up, it would have passed without comment. The altercation displayed Russell's sensitive side. Despite getting even, the incident still played on Russell's mind – so much so that he felt compelled to ask friends who had seen it what they thought. 'I've been told since by numerous people whose opinion I respect – Noel Gallagher, for instance, and Carl Barat – that [Geldof] misjudged the room, and it was just embarrassing and awkward. There was a part of me that needed that confirmation,' he told Barbara Ellen in *The Observer*.

Later, his tone softened, although he still named his retort as one of the ten funniest moments of the year. Months on, when asked by *The Sun* if the former Boomtown Rats frontman had apologized, Russell said: 'No, he hasn't. But I admired him before and, to a degree, I still do.'

It was not to be the only drama of the night. New Order's Peter Hook came on stage to present the Best Live Band prize to Franz Ferdinand. When he heard they had not turned up, Hook took it upon himself to proclaim the Kaiser Chiefs the winners.

In a bid to head off a diplomatic incident, Russell was forced to intervene, saying: 'Now we've got to ask the Kaiser Chiefs, do they really think it's right to accept an award voted for by readers – readers who voted for Franz Ferdinand?' The situation descended into further chaos when the Kaiser Chiefs elected to pass it on to the Cribs. Overexcited at the prospect of getting his hands on the trophy, Cribs lead singer Ryan Jarman took a running jump, tried to make a grab for the prize, missed ... and landed slap-bang in the middle of the band's table, smashing glass everywhere and suffering a gash on the back of his leg.

It was the sort of mad stunt Russell himself would have pulled a few years ago. Yet now, standing just a few feet away, he managed to remain calm and collected. 'That may have looked chaotic, but that took hours of careful planning for that young man to cover himself in booze,' he deadpanned. 'That was a thrilling moment of live television there. I just hope that young man's spine survived the antics.'

The buzz was building around Russell. Broadcasters were convinced they had found their holy grail: the 'It boy' who was sexy, funny and – most crucial of all – could appeal to the key sixteen- to twenty-four-year-old demographic. Russell was the new Jonathan Ross, but edgier, thinner and more risqué. At the offices of John Noel Management, the phone didn't stop ringing. In March 2006, Russell flew to Miami to make a Channel 4 documentary on the Raelians – a cult who believed that sexual pleasures should be freely practised for the good of mankind. Russell was also flattered when he was picked by Ricky Gervais to host a comedy night in aid of the Teenage Cancer Trust at the Royal Albert Hall.

The first TV offer to come to fruition was from MTV. After seeing his work on *Big Brother's Big Mouth*, bosses at the music-video station were ready to welcome him back into the fold. Calling Russell their 'wayward prodigal son', the channel's representatives said they were willing to forgive and forget his past misdemeanours, before adding: 'We must be mad.' For Russell, it was conclusive proof that he had repaired the damage he had done to his career. He responded in an equally tongue-in-cheek manner, saying: 'I am better now, I'll be no trouble, I promise. I won't steal stationery, misuse the photocopier or consume mind-bending drinks whilst on telly.' *One Leicester Square* was to be a celebrity-interview show, shot at a new studio on the site of the old Home nightclub in London. It was the first regular programme to be broadcast from the studio.

Filmed in front of an audience of forty, the show featured celebrity interviews, comedy sketches and musical performances. Just as he had with *Big Brother's Big Mouth*, Russell created an atmosphere in which it felt like anything could happen. It played to Russell's strengths and his ability to take the most inane celebrity answers off on a tangent and make them interesting. He also resurrected an idea he had thought up for *Comedy Lab*, and included a section where the audience asked for advice on their personal problems.

The first guests on the opening programme on 2 April were The Streets and the Stereophonics. The show hit its stride a few weeks later, when it scooped Tom Cruise's only British TV interview to promote *Mission: Impossible III*. Russell was fascinated by Cruise because of the sheer size of his celebrity status. 'Talking to Tom Cruise is like interviewing Coca-Cola or oxygen,' he said in an interview with Ben Thompson for *The Daily Telegraph*. 'When fame reaches these preposterous levels, it becomes more like an abstract idea.' If he was star-struck when Cruise walked up to him in the corridor, shook him warmly by the hand and addressed him by name, he didn't show it. Instead, he did his best to shoot down the carefully managed Hollywood patter, laughing at the 'staged bonhomie' between Cruise and Jamie Foxx, and commenting that 'they promoted each other's films and albums as a token of their friendship, like a couple of glamorous chimpanzees'.

Russell was also making inroads into another medium at this time. He had already tried his hand at radio, on XFM with his mates Matt and Will four years earlier, during their *Re:Brand* days. (They had been fired while they were still on air, for reading out porn from the letters page of the *Sunday Sport*.) So when BBC 6 Music DJ Nemone had gone on a Christmas break at the end of 2005, their mutual agent John Noel was quick to see a showcase in which Russell could resurrect his radio career. John also represented Ricky Gervais's sidekick, Karl Pilkington. Karl was already famous from XFM, where he was a comic foil to Gervais and Stephen Merchant, thanks to his dour northern delivery and oblique view of life. It was suggested that Russell and Karl form a double act and fill in for three days.

They were the ultimate odd couple. But the yin of Karl's miserable-git schtick and the yang of Russell's Essex-boy cockiness worked well. The shows managed to be low-key and utterly absurd at the same time. Karl summed up their partnership by saying in a press release: 'He's the good-looking bloke, all long hair, heroin addiction and bad times. Everything he's about, I'm like, "That doesn't happen," and he doesn't understand me.' Russell agreed that they couldn't be more different. Karl viewed life from 'the unique perspective of a man who once fell off a horse at a school fête and has since eschewed all experience, preferring to spend his life worrying in a cupboard. We will quarrel about social etiquette, monkey society, dating and safety regulations at school fêtes.'

The three shows had gone down well; indeed, 6 Music and Radio 2 controller Lesley Douglas liked what she heard so much that it was agreed that Russell and Karl should fill a regular Sunday lunchtime slot. Starting from 9 April 2006, their programme was originally billed as 'Sunday School', with the pair picking a random subject about which to educate the masses each week – plus Karl explaining the story behind a song.

However, the partnership was to prove short-lived. Within two weeks, Karl was gone. Rumours immediately circulated that he had walked out, with the gossip-mongers suggesting that Russell had said something on air to upset him. But given that most of Karl's career had been spent being mercilessly ribbed by Ricky Gervais and Stephen Merchant, it seemed unlikely he should suddenly develop a sensitive side.

Instead, as Russell's new sidekick, his long-time mate Trevor Lock, later explained, Karl had bowed out because the podcast of the programme was in direct competition with a show he did with Gervais and Merchant, which was number one in the charts. Speculation about any serious rift was laid to rest when Karl briefly continued to produce the show for a while, and even made an appearance on the programme on 5 May, phoning in one of his deadpan holiday reports from Lyme Regis.

Russell wasted no time drafting in his friend and co-writer Matt Morgan, together with Trevor. Russell had stayed in touch with the latter since they had first met at the Edinburgh Festival in 2000, and he had invited him to perform at many of the stand-up nights he had organized both before and after he was in rehab. They had since become close pals.

Russell was still clearly the star of the show. He would be at the microphone, with the text number in front of him, amid a chaotic mess of papers, broadcasting his thoughts like he was delivering an improvised stand-up gig. The programme was light on records, although Russell's favourite band The Smiths featured prominently, much to Matt's chagrin. It was heavy on nostalgia, with Matt and Russell often relating their tales of debauchery from their MTV and *Re:Brand* days. Trevor took on the equivalent of Karl's character in the Gervais podcasts, as the bullied idiot savant.

During the three-hour slot, Russell would veer between hectoring Trevor and telling him to 'eat his fudge', and allowing Matt to disclose many of his most depraved secrets. Usually, the show started with Russell giving an update on its performance in the podcasts chart. He was obsessed that the programme should do well, publicizing it at every opportunity. He was delighted when it finally got to number two.

When Russell had appeared on Jonathan Ross's Radio 2 show in March, Ross had been taken with Russell's buccaneering new image and the pair hit it off well. But when the time came for Russell to appear on Ross's Friday night TV show in May, he was nervous. He was already being touted as a possible successor and feared the older man would consider him 'a usurper that will have to be slain'.

Russell knew this was his moment. Back in Essex, Babs was certainly telling neighbours it was. One recalled how she had pulled up in her car and told her: 'Russell's made it – he's going to be on *Jonathan Ross!*' She would be proved right.

For the sake of those who had never laid eyes on him, the opening minutes saw Ross helpfully summarizing Russell's look as 'Max Wall meets Pete Doherty via Lily Savage with a little bit of Keith Richards thrown in for good measure'. Russell gave it his all. Looking back on it, compared to his more assured TV performances, it was clear he was on edge. He shifted around on the couch, grinning manically, crossing and uncrossing his legs. As he was apt to do when he was in the presence of another Alpha male, he also became as camp as possible.

Yet Russell knew that this was his chance to pitch his brand. He drove the message home by stressing his unique selling points, describing himself as 'an S&M Willy Wonka' and 'a

Dickensian pimp'. His language was at its most florid and Victorian, to give stories of how he had been arrested for buying porn at an all-night garage maximum impact.

It was a crash course in Russell – a flirtatious, dizzying performance that left many people unable to keep up, some of them totally confused, and most of them wanting more. By the end of the fifteen-minute interview, Russell Brand was a star.

CHAPTER TWELVE

SUMMER OF LOVE

'If you're in a room with a woman, what's the most interesting thing you can do?'

— RUSSELL IN THE *EVENING STANDARD*, AUGUST 2006

When Russell was invited to bare his soul for a new book of verse by stand-up comedians, *That Which Is Not Said*, the subject he chose was his womanizing. His poem 'Feed Me' explored the gap between the fantasy of having 'all them girls' and the reality of getting too many.

In the verse, he answers a man who enviously compares his ability to have the pick of any woman he wants to being like a kid in a sweet shop. But then Russell goes on to imagine the ultimate consequence of gorging continually. He pictures the attraction of the sweets dimming, all that temptation stripped of appeal. He memorably evokes an image of the sweet-shop floor being scattered with wrappers, 'like a Columbine on Wonka's factory floor'. Humour is given the last laugh – 'What wouldn't I give for a sprout' – but the protagonist's eventual death by diabetes reveals Russell was perhaps all too aware of the danger of his ongoing sex addiction and womanizing.

The analogy between gorging on women and gorging on sweets was an interesting one for Russell, who had once been bulimic and used food as a way to assert control over an unhappy life. Since rehab, sex had taken over from drugs as Russell's preferred method of escaping from reality. The oblivion of an orgasm consumed him in the same way as heroin had once done.

Unable now to drink after performances, sex had become his way of relaxing after the adrenalin high. As he told Bruce

Dessau of the *Evening Standard*: 'I'm sure there is a degree of compulsive behaviour, but if you are in a room with a woman, what is the most interesting thing you can do? There aren't many things as diverting as an orgasm. You can be on a mountain top and appreciate beauty and nature, but those things take a lot of effort and there's the immediacy of sex and orgasm, and previously drugs, which make me cling on to them.'

Summer 2006 was to all intents and purposes Russell's summer of love, kicking off with his (in)famous affair with supermodel Kate Moss. In the following weeks, barely a day went by without some new quote, rumour or liaison. Russell would be variously dubbed 'a legendary swordsman', 'a sextraterrestrial' and 'a sex insect' – a term he didn't like because he didn't think insects were sufficiently alluring. Russell's sex life was to become such an accepted part of the national consciousness that at the end of August, *The Sun* printed a cheeky come-on for its readers, asking: 'Have you bonked Russell this week?'

Russell had always been highly sexed. His first infatuation was at the age of six, with the busty neighbour opposite, who had nipped over to his house to have a bath. He later scribbled nipples on some holiday photos of her in an orange bikini – and used the shots as pornography. As a boy, he had liked to watch *The Incredible Hulk* – because when the hero flexed his chest muscles, they looked like a pair of breasts.

Nor did his taste in women become more sophisticated with age. He confessed that the females he would most like to take to a desert island would be porn stars or Page Three girls. He named Linsey Dawn McKenzie or Michelle Marsh as his ideal castaways: 'Big sluts who would abuse me all day and night.' It said a lot about Russell's desires that his favourite sexual encounter was with an Australian lap dancer. He described her as 'extremely tall, with these sumptuous breasts and a vagina that just devoured me in every way. My life just froze that night, trapped in this oasis of pure physical pleasure.'

Looks-wise, Kate Moss was the exact opposite of the women Russell usually went for. But with his dirty rock-star image, he was very much her type – and she was accustomed to getting her own way. Normally, skinny flat-chested women did nothing for him. However, Russell found it hard not to have his head turned by the attentions of Britain's most celebrated supermodel.

The pair were introduced by a mutual friend, Sadie Frost. Russell had become friendly with the former actress and ex-wife of Jude Law, as well as other members of the Primrose Hill set, when he had lived in the area. The same agent, John Noel, represented both him and Sadie. They had plenty of other things in common, too. Like Russell, Sadie had gone to the Italia Conti stage school, albeit a few years before him, and both attended north London AA meetings.

At the time, Kate was still in love with her on-off ex, heroin addict and Libertines star Pete Doherty. But after she was pictured in the *Daily Mirror* snorting cocaine, it was generally agreed that she should try to find a boyfriend not involved in drugs. When Sadie suggested that they check out Russell's gig in the theatre over the Hen and Chickens, a pub on Highbury Corner, Kate leapt at the chance. She had seen Russell on TV just a few days earlier and had, according to one witness, 'squealed with delight'.

The Monday night gig was a couple of days after Russell had lit up *Friday Night with Jonathan Ross*. He could almost feel his career taking off and his confidence was high. When he first glimpsed Kate at the bar, her hair was down and she was wearing a pair of black skinny jeans not dissimilar to his own, and a blue bolero jacket. As Sadie introduced them, the mutual interest was palpable. No doubt briefed that his chances of pulling Britain's top model were good, Russell delivered the killer chat-up line: 'I know you just want to shag me, but you are going to have to wait until after the show.'

Up on the stage, Russell was on peak form. It was a warm-up gig for his Edinburgh Festival *Shame* production, which he planned to take to the Fringe that summer. He paced the floor barefoot as he regaled the audience with some of his most humiliating incidents. For one story, he disclosed how he had suddenly broken into an American accent while talking dirty in bed. Far from being put off, Kate was mesmerized.

Immediately after the show, all three jumped in a cab to head for aristocratic nightspot Annabel's in Berkeley Square. The occasion was a celebrity auction in aid of the Hoping Foundation, supporting Palestinian refugees. Jade Jagger and Rupert Everett were among the glitzy crowd. Prizes for the main event of the evening included a round of golf with Hugh Grant. Pick of the night was a kiss with Kate. After a bout of competitive bidding, retail billionaire Philip Green offered to pay an astonishing £60,000. With his wife in attendance, however, Sir Philip passed on the prize to glamorous socialite Jemima Khan.

As Russell looked on, Kate gave Jemima a deep, sensual kiss. One eyewitness said: 'We thought it was going to be a kiss on the cheek. It lasted just over sixty seconds. A few people were shocked, but everyone was laughing afterwards.' It was clear the party was not over when Sadie and Kate caught a cab home – but merely took two circuits round the block to try to shake off photographers before coming back to pick up Russell.

Reports that Russell was Kate's new man hit the papers almost immediately. Just two days later, a source told *The Sun*: 'Kate finds Russell hilarious and he has the sort of rock-star looks she's attracted to. But they have deeper things in common. He is recovering from drugs, booze and sex addiction problems. Kate has been through her cocaine scandal and is getting over junkie Pete. So they have a lot to talk about. They spent the night together and have been on the phone since. All Kate's friends think he is the perfect man for her. She's found someone who also used to go wild and remains successful, but is trying to live a clean life.'

Despite his track record with women, Russell could still be insecure about the opposite sex. The fact that the most talked-about woman in Britain was clearly interested in him felt like validation.

In the early stages, Kate wanted the relationship kept as quiet as possible, especially while she was still unsure of her feelings for Pete. She briefed Russell not to say a word. Nonetheless, it was observed that whenever Russell got so much as a one-word text from her, he yelped with joy.

To Kate's dismay, it took only a few days for their fling to be confirmed – by a photograph of a dishevelled Russell streaking out of her St John's Wood home, the morning after they had spent the night together.

For the previous three weeks, a team of photographers from picture agency Big Pictures had been trailing Russell. 'Russell kept talking about his sex life on the show, so we were keeping an eye on him because he was always going to be a good tabloid story,' recalls agency boss Darryn Lyons. The previous night, Kate and Russell had gone out in a group and been trailed back to her house. When the couple awoke, the photographers were still there waiting for the lovebirds to emerge.

Kate had to catch a plane from Stansted Airport. The idea was for Kate to leave by the front door and distract the snappers, while Russell vanished out the back. The paparazzi, however, had them outnumbered. As Kate came out to get into her car, a member of the Big Pictures team spotted Russell scaling the rear wall and trying to make a run for it. The subsequent snapshot of an unkempt Russell in his sunglasses, trying to button up his shirt, was to be one of the tabloid images of the summer. As Kate saw Russell get hosed down by the photographers, she was left shaking her head in despair.

Darryn said: 'It was a fantastic hit. It was one of those real hide-and-seek pictures you get when someone is caught out having an affair. You could just tell from the body language that something was going on. They had planned to escape, but not together and they blew it.' The next day, the photo appeared in both *The Sun* and the *Daily Mirror*.

A few days later, Darryn appeared on *Big Brother's Big Mouth* and took some printouts of the shots with him. 'Apparently, Russell was quite pissed off at the time, but he managed to make a good joke of it for the telly and ripped them all up and threw them around. He told me he loved watching my show *Paparazzi*, so I would have thought he would have known better than to jump over walls. But I think the picture seriously helped in the making of Russell Brand. He was building his press and publicity on being a philanderer, and that picture said it all.'

Certainly, show-business editors couldn't believe their luck. Not only did they have a photo of Russell fleeing a tryst with Kate Moss, looking like Casanova reinvented for the new millennium, but a quick search of old press cuttings turned up magazine articles written by Russell, in which he freely confessed to being a sex addict and user of prostitutes.

Furthermore, Russell's arrival on the scene was a welcome break from Kate's revolving-door relationship with Doherty. Tired of the is-she-isn't-she-going-out-with-him stories, this looked like the start of a much more interesting chapter. Doherty was a pasty-faced rock star who took drugs. Russell looked like a rock star, but had given up the drugs. Moreover, he was funny, outrageous and on TV.

Yet the liaison was to be short-lived. For one thing, Kate was still in love with the ex-Libertine, and it was proving an uncomfortable love triangle. Russell had already met Doherty the year before, at the 2005 *NME* Awards. It had been one of the rare occasions when he had been lost for words. This time, it was Russell's turn to be shocked by drug-taking in the loos. 'I went for a wee and Pete went to the toilet because he's a drug addict. He started cooking up and I said, "Pete, you should probably do that in a cubicle because it's very illegal." So I ended up holding his spoon for him because he didn't have enough hands to do it. Then, after he'd shot up, he sprayed "QPR" on the wall in his own blood and I went, "Oh, are you a big [Queens Park] Rangers fan, then?" because I didn't know what to say.' Russell was also a very close friend of ex-Libertine Carl Barat, who had been responsible for ejecting Pete from the band.

The day after the picture of Russell fleeing Kate's house appeared, Pete turned up to see her, vowing to get clean if that would win her back. The papers the next day were full of photographs that claimed to show Kate with a black eye. Kate's people, however, strongly denied any such allegation, saying it was simply the way the pictures had been taken. Whatever the truth, the supermodel was clearly irritated to find her love life being so closely chronicled on camera. A few hours after Pete left, she kicked a photographer and stamped on his lens cap. Just as it looked like he might lose Kate to Russell, Doherty checked into a rehab clinic.

If Kate's continued involvement with Pete didn't sound the death knell for her fling with Russell, then an incident a few days later definitely did. The following Sunday night, 28 May, Russell was approached by a female reporter at the ABC bar in Crystal Palace, where he had been performing a stand-up gig.

Caught on the hop, Russell told her: 'Kate's a great girl. Things are going well for me at the moment, but I hope I don't get caught running out of her house again. That was embarrassing. I'm single, if not a little promiscuous!'

When Kate read it in the *Daily Mirror*, she was humiliated. 'She accused him of being paid thousands and making money off her name, ranting, raving, calling him a twat,' said a friend of the model. 'When she found out he'd had loads of work offers since then, she went even more ballistic. Thinking that people are making money out of her is one of her big hobby horses. She's always claiming people have sold stories about her for £500,000 when they're not true. Russell made a total fool out of her.'

If further confirmation were needed that any spark between them had died out, it came in the *Sunday Mirror* on 4 June. Russell was appalled to open the paper and read an account of an evening he had spent with a girl, who turned out to be a reporter.

Russell had started talking to journalist Nikhita Mahajan at the bar after a gig at the Lowdown Comedy Club in Great Portland Street the previous Wednesday, and had invited her back to his Gospel Oak flat. Once there, by his own admission he did his best to talk her into bed and was rather confused when she steadfastly resisted his charms. When he realized nothing was on the cards, he promptly called her a cab.

Though bewildered by her reaction, Russell thought no more of it – until Nikhita penned a description of the evening for that weekend's paper. In the article, she painted Russell as a whining Romeo, who dismissed Kate Moss as 'irrelevant', before adding: 'I prefer women with a bit of meat on them anyway.'

Leaving aside how it affected his relationship with Kate, Russell was stung by the depiction of his seduction technique. The story made him sound desperate and pathetic. 'I am a sexy wild man and you're nice and soft … let me hold you,' ran the report. 'You must trust me. I'm part of the universe. There's no point in not listening to me. It's like trying to fight biology. If you let me kiss you, you'll feel better. Kiss me, you'll feel great. I'm not asking you to do anything, I'm asking you to stop preventing something. You don't have to be active, you just have to let go. Please let me see your sexy body. Please let me touch you and stuff. How can you resist?'

Russell was horrified. On his 6 Music show the same day, he addressed the story. He did not deny the incident had happened, but did quibble with the detail, in particular the claim that he had referred to himself as 'a sexy wildman'. He said it was entrapment of the worst kind. 'Remember, I am single. I don't have no children. So if, after a gig, some girl swans up to me, I think: "Ooh, nice. Might be exciting. Something to do."' However, he acknowledged that there were several trademark Brand wooing techniques featured in the article, including his insistence that Nikhita should make the most of her fleeting youth and seize the moment to sleep with him.

After dissecting the story on air, Russell tried to make light of it by putting on a girl's voice and phoning the *Sunday Mirror* news desk. He pretended to have an exposé about how Russell Brand liked to frolic in green tights in bed, and dress up as Robin Hood. The reporter quickly guessed it was a wind-up and hung up.

Despite his attempt to put a humorous edge on it, behind the scenes his people were furious. His agent John Noel was so incensed that he said he would no longer deal with any Mirror Group papers.

These experiences had taught Russell a lesson. In interviews, Kate Moss quickly became the one and only area into which Russell would not stray. Journalists, who were thrilled to have an interview subject who seemed willing to cover every topic from orgies to drug-taking, suddenly hit an immovable brick wall if they so much as mentioned the supermodel's name. As he told the *Evening Standard*: 'I am saying nothing. I'll tell people anything, but I don't think it's fair to talk about others. My default setting is to tell everyone everything, but now I'm in a position where it affects others.'

Though he was no longer prepared to speak about it, the liaison had nevertheless propelled Russell into the celebrity stratosphere. Within two days of the tabloid snap appearing, he was number two on the *OK!* magazine celebrity chart, behind Paul McCartney. He was on his way to becoming the most talked-about media figure of the summer. To begin with, at least, Russell seemed quite happy to fan the flames of his notoriety with yet more confessions, letting slip that he had once pleasured himself with the nozzle of a vacuum cleaner called Henry.

It coincided with the publication of his self-penned six-point plan for seducing women. His biggest tip was 'know your brand identity', writing in *GQ*: 'Be in tune with your USP [unique selling point]. For me, the idea of a gauche philandering adventurer works quite well. I have the hair of a gauche philandering adventurer, the patter of a gauche philandering adventurer and offer gauche philandering adventures. The brand is consistent.'

As soon as the Kate Moss story hit the press, news desks started to receive calls from women who said they had slept with Russell. Considering that Russell claimed to bed up to five women a day at his peak, the eight kiss-and-tells that appeared over the following months meant he got off lightly.

First out of the starting blocks was Becki Seddiki, who appeared in the *Sunday Mirror* on 28 May with her account of how Russell had picked her up in the street eighteen months previously. Russell did not quibble with her assertion that he was sex-obsessed, admitting he was 'guilty as charged'. But he was hurt by her suggestion that he was only interested in himself in bed. 'That's not true. I do like to satisfy women – out of a boastful arrogance. You feel more confident when you make a woman fully satisfied.'

A few days later, Makosi's review of Russell during their six-week affair was kinder. 'He was an insatiable lover and, while he wasn't the most well endowed, he knew exactly what he was doing,' she told *Closer*. 'He wasn't selfish and knew exactly how to please a woman.'

Next up, on 11 June, was veteran kiss-and-tell merchant Cassie Sumner, who had broken up with Russell in January after a two-month relationship. This time, however, her story was being told by 'a pal'. She revealed how they had split up when she found used condoms in the bedroom, and because she felt unable to comply with his request to have a threesome with a hooker.

Russell confessed on his 6 Music show that he had gone out with Cassie for a while, but denied her claims that he had asked her for sex with a £40-a-time prostitute, reasoning that 'it was not an area where you would want to be looking for a bargain'.

In August, Elke Heywood came forward with a recollection of a night she had spent with Russell nine years earlier. Elke had been two years above Russell at Italia Conti, remembering him as a 'skinny lippy schoolboy'. Since then, her hopes of a show-business career had not advanced, and she was now reduced to singing in an Abba tribute band. It meant that *People*'s subeditors had a field day with the story, telling how Russell had made her go 'Mamma Mia' when she saw his pasty white body and scream 'Gimme Gimme Gimme (Another Man After Midnight)' after his performance lasted barely a minute.

Again, Russell didn't dispute they had sex, but he was upset by her description. Elke claimed Russell 'pounded on top of me like a rabid dog, looking at me with those crazed eyes'. As far as Russell had been aware, it had been a perfectly ordinary sexual encounter.

By the end of the summer, exposés on Russell were becoming so common that they were no longer news. Glamour girl Coralie Robinson, another veteran on the kiss-and-tell circuit, told the *News of the World*: 'Me and Russell are having fun, it's true. But we're not seeing each other exclusively.'

When several more girls came out of the woodwork to talk about how busy Russell had been at the Edinburgh Festival, the stories hardly made a half page.

Instead, it had become newsworthy when a woman *didn't* sleep with Russell. Myleene Klass was the first person reported to resist his charms, because she was engaged. Socialite Tamara Beckwith also gave him short shrift, according to the *Daily Star*; both Russell and Tamara, though, confirmed they had never met each other.

Russell's worst rejection was to come from Dannii Minogue. In June, the singer had gone on *One Leicester Square* to promote her new album *The Hits & Beyond*, and Russell complimented her on her breasts while on air. The exchange looked good-natured enough, but afterwards Dannii let rip to the *Daily Mirror*: 'He is completely crazy and a bit of a vile predator. I certainly don't think he has cured his sex addiction, that's for sure. He wouldn't take no for an answer. He always goes that step too far. Never quite far enough to slap his face, but usually too far.'

Playing up the role of the offended innocent for all it was worth, she added: 'Throughout the whole interview, he kept making shocking remarks that I can't even repeat. Just uttering the words would make me blush.'

Once more, Russell felt so wronged that he felt compelled to defend himself. 'That's out of order,' he said. 'I'm just a man. I'm a bit chatty. I like girls, you know? "Vile predator"? If that's the language you're going to use about someone who really ought to be described as "having a bit of an eye for the ladies", then what sort of language are you left with for Peter Sutcliffe and Ian Huntley?' He stormed: 'I don't remember giving her my phone number, but if I did, it is because she needs support with her fragile mental state.'

The subject was also touched on during his 6 Music show, in which he said he was a bit surprised by Dannii's apparent prudery, considering pictures of her kissing and fondling a naked lap dancer had recently appeared in the *News of the World*. His friend Noel Gallagher also leapt to Russell's defence, saying: 'What programme did she think she was going on – *Newsnight*?'

Even when out of the papers, Russell was however living up to his reputation. He would repeatedly check for flirtatious texts and gave his number out relatively freely to any attractive women who caught his eye. One of the recipients was columnist and TV personality Vanessa Feltz, who had become a friend since being invited as a guest on *Big Brother's Big Mouth*. It was all purely for fun, but she admitted she couldn't get enough 'titillating texts' from Russell, adding: 'Long may they continue.'

By the end of the summer, Russell had two phones. There was Cooper, his nickname for his mobile, and his 'tart phone', which he used to conduct his love life and carry on his numerous textual flirtations. When he saw a woman he liked, he would bite his fist. He confessed that his greatest deadly sin was Lust, adding that when he saw someone beautiful, he thought: 'Oh! I could give you *such* a cuddle!' As far as Russell was concerned, he was just doing what came naturally. He had a surplus of energy, and sex was one of life's great pleasures.

As the year wore on, he liked to paint himself as a tortured Casanova who, like Prince Charming, was only trying other women for size until he found the one who would cure him. He did feel he was being unfairly portrayed. 'The kind of sex I like, it ain't unpleasant. I like gentle, adoring, tactile sex, not disposable, bloody sleazy sex,' he told the *Sunday Herald*. 'It should be natural and nice.' He wasn't addicted, he insisted. He just liked the feeling and he was 'a promiscuous singleton' doing no harm.

It was easy for him to blame the tabloids for harping on about it. But he was just as expansive on the subject in the broadsheets. As Russell told *The Observer*: 'I like to think of myself as a conduit of natural forces. After all, the most natural thing in the world is for people to fuck, isn't it? So all you have to do is remove all the reasons why women don't actually go through with it, like pride and reputation. You just have to unpick the conditions stopping women going straight to bed with you.'

After discovering that his womanizing gave him the fame he craved, Russell now found it was getting in his way.

CHAPTER THIRTEEN

LIFE AS A STAR

'I can't stand all those people who become famous and then start saying it's a normal job – and it just happened – as if they were a plumber or something. I have always wanted to be famous.'

— RUSSELL IN *GQ* MAGAZINE,
OCTOBER 2006

The walls of Ron Brand's living room are a shrine to his son. There are collages of pictures of Russell, baby photos, reviews and publicity shots. In a frame, there is also the handwritten poem Russell wrote for his nan, Jen, when she died in 1999.

Ron had always been fiercely proud of Russell. He had not always been the most responsible dad, but he had tried to make up for it in his own way, and had constantly encouraged Russell to reach for the top. True, he had not been around as much as he might have been in the early years – and Russell had never forgiven him for it. But he had paid for Russell to attend Italia Conti, supported him at his earliest stand-up gigs and helped him put on his first show in Edinburgh.

They now had a matey relationship based on a shared interest in women and West Ham. They had also recently gone into business together, somewhat bizarrely buying a greeting-cards company belonging to the glamour model Jordan. It hadn't been an easy ride, but their father/son dynamic was getting there.

So it was especially painful for Ron when he became the first casualty of Russell's fame. When he was approached by the *Daily Mirror* at his home in Farnham, where he was a director of a communications firm, in June 2006, Ron was wary. Russell had just been thrown into the spotlight thanks to his liaison with Kate Moss, and now everyone wanted to know all there was to know about him.

Politely, the paper's reporter asked if there were any childhood pictures he was prepared to share. Ron declined the request to show any baby snaps, but chatted amiably about how proud he was of his son and what Russell had been like as a child. Beaming with pride, he said: 'I'm reluctant to use the word "genius", but Russell is different. He has something special, a drive. Russell will go to Hollywood. He's a talent.'

Russell had warned his family that if they were approached by the media, they were to say nothing. But always a great talker, Ron's natural exuberance simply got the better of him. When his quotes appeared as part of a wider analysis of Russell's background, some of his remarks touched a nerve, and were interpreted by Russell's mum Babs as claiming more credit for his upbringing than it was felt he deserved.

The following month, Russell told the *Sunday Herald* that he had cut off contact with his father. 'I'd specifically asked him not to [speak to the press] and he said things that upset my mum. He didn't pay maintenance to my mum. He was not a good father and he is now not a part of my life.'

Devastated, Ron still continued to text Russell, sending him a thought for the day. 'It really is very, very sad,' said a family member. 'Ron wasn't perfect as a father – and I think there's some truth in the fact that because his own dad died young he didn't have an example to follow. But I have seen Ron with tears in his eyes because he is so proud of Russell. It would break Jen's heart if she knew about this.'

Although he had hankered after fame all his life, his first six months at the top were still a rollercoaster for Russell. He had lusted after celebrity for as long as he could remember. Now, every morning, he would go through a stack of newspapers – in Matt Morgan's words, 'like a rat through a sack' – looking for stories and pictures about himself. Matt added: 'He doesn't blink.'

To begin with, Russell loved the fact that he had finally

made it. 'I can't stand all those people who become famous and then start saying it's a normal job – as if they were a plumber or something,' he told *GQ*. 'I have always wanted to be famous.' He added that he adored 'the recognition and the sense of power and the notoriety'.

Certainly, in interviews, every journalist who turned up ready to be annoyed was enchanted. Vicky Allen of the *Sunday Herald* had her expectations confounded, saying that Russell 'seems simply likeable and intellectually engaging company'. Piers Morgan also assumed he'd find Russell 'irritating and pointless', only to discover he was 'charming, articulate and very, very funny'. Robert Crampton of *The Times* admitted it was hard not to like him. One female reporter was so enamoured by him she was rumoured to have ended up in bed with him after the interview.

Russell also had the respect of journalists because it was clear that he was more than capable of putting pen to paper himself. Throughout his career, he had found it easy to translate his skill with words on to the page, writing quirky, confessional pieces for *Time Out* and *Elle*. After he wrote for *The Guardian* on the football World Cup, the paper gave him a weekly column. Often, Russell would stray perilously close to the deadline. To save time, he would dictate his thoughts off the top of his head into his Dictaphone, for his personal assistant to transcribe.

For one memorable article for *The Observer Music Monthly*, Russell flew to Cologne to interview Rolling Stone Keith Richards. Russell was hampered by the fact that he got no more than twenty-five words with the great man. Half of that was saying hello and goodbye. Portraying himself as a tongue-tied Frank Spencer figure, Russell stretched the meeting into a three-page essay on the gap between expectation and reality when you meet rock icons. He was merciless about the Stones' PR machine, observing, 'The band, their image and their legacy are defended more fiercely than the monarchy.' One reader called the feature 'the finest twenty-first-century profile of Keith Richards – a dozen times more revealing than the usual puff piece that drops out of rock critics' bowels every time the Stones pull into town.' Others were a bit perplexed as to why Russell had gone into so much detail about his personal toilet habits in the story.

Yet there were pitfalls. Russell found that the risqué allusions he made in his stand-up could look in poor taste in print. In his World Cup column, he compared a penalty-happy referee to mass murderer Michael Ryan, who killed sixteen people on a rampage through Hungerford in 1987. During a live routine, it wouldn't have raised an eyebrow. Two days later, *The Guardian* hastily apologized for the 'totally inappropriate and offensive metaphor'.

With his new image in place, Russell approached *Big Brother 7* with renewed enthusiasm. Thanks to *One Leicester Square* and his 6 Music show, he was attracting a cult following, and he finally felt people were getting the message. The last episode of *Celebrity Big Brother's Big Mouth* on E4 in January had managed to achieve better ratings than Channel 4. As Russell pointed out: 'You can't argue with statistics.'

It was his third year on the programme and he still loved to revel in dissecting the activities of the housemates. As he told Channel 4's Benjie Goodhart: 'While it is on, we all live next door to that house. Of course, you can look at it and say it's exploitative, it's sensational, it's salacious, but what's always amazed me about it is that humanity always emerges.'

The timing of the new series could not have been better for Russell. It kicked off on 18 May 2006, just as tabloid interest was soaring following the first reports of his fling with Kate Moss. For this run of the show, Russell was to have even more scope for his comedy. There was now a host of absurd animals for him to spar with. They included a Scouse whale who didn't like *Big Brother*, but insisted he had a right to be on the programme anyway; and Rosebud, a well-spoken horse, who reported back to Russell on the activities of the 'Womanizing Circuit', an imaginary group of Lotharios, which included David Walliams, Dean Gaffney and Michael Greco.

Little Jon Connell also got an expanded role. Jon, a boffinish schoolboy from Liverpool, had first featured as a panellist and expert on *Efourum* when he was fifteen. A pupil at Merchant Taylors' private school, he was such a fanatic that he had entered a competition and won the couch from *Big Brother 4*. Now, for *Big Brother 7*, Jon was invited to take part in a regular segment where he appeared in a scientist's lab coat to put up complex charts and models to illustrate his theories on the housemates. The gag was that Russell would either rip up the chart or kick it over. The cast was completed by Little Paul Scholes, a talking doll of the Manchester United football player, who was also knocked over by Russell.

For each show, Russell did a monologue about his 'ball bags'. He had been shouting about his ball bags since his days at MTV. Now his testicles were not only attributed with two distinct personalities – the 'younger, shyer bag' and the 'older, more confident bag' – but also with their own careers. Using various puns based on the word 'bags', Russell charted their celebrity adventures. He would sign off with a dramatic flourish and his catchphrase: 'The swines!'

The new concepts were surreal, but somehow they worked. *The Observer* reviewer Andrew Anthony said of Russell: 'His leaps of imagination are unconstrained by any fear that the audience might not be able to follow him. He just seems to say whatever comes into his mind and, more often than not, it's inspired.'

It would not have been a series of *Big Brother* without Russell being linked to a housemate. Physically, Imogen Thomas was Russell's type: dark eyes and hair, with a curvaceous figure. He was rumoured to have wined and dined the former Miss Wales for two weeks, after calling her out of the blue. He was also spotted giving her a guided tour of the MTV studios and advice on how to break into TV presenting. According to the *Sunday Mirror*: 'What was surprising was that he seemed to be really keen on her. He was hanging on her every word and treating her like a lady.'

Meanwhile, since its launch in April, Russell's 6 Music radio show had proved a huge hit with listeners. It had risen to number two in the podcasts chart, an achievement of which Russell was extremely proud. The programme flowed well, thanks to the banter between Russell, Matt and Trevor. But invariably, fans also tuned in to hear Russell's latest outrageous confessions. They ranged from how he, Matt and Trevor had gone to have colonic irrigation as a team-building exercise, to how a glimpse of David Walliams's skin-tight shorts had shamed Russell into stuffing some socks down his Y-fronts.

Russell's friend Noel Gallagher had become a regular contributor. Noel had been a guest on *One Leicester Square* and Russell found him 'really clever, funny, down-to-earth and thoughtful'. Now, most weeks, Noel would ring in, providing the same sort of dour Mancunian humour that Karl Pilkington had done, but with rock-star attitude. Unexpectedly, the Oasis singer delivered many of the show's best one-liners. When a listener emailed to ask if Noel still had a mattress he had sold him a couple of years ago, Russell joked it must have seen some 'hellish exploits'. 'I beg your pardon? Hellish?' Noel deadpanned. 'Just straight-up erotica.'

Predictably, the show was not without its controversies. One of Russell's close friends was Ade Adepitan, best known as one of the 'wheelchair dancers' in the BBC1 ident. Ade had contracted polio when he was a baby. As a member of the British Paralympic basketball team, he had gone on to win a bronze medal at the 2004 Athens Paralympics and had been awarded an MBE in 2005 for his services to disabled sport. Russell and Ade had been mates for four years. They shared the same agent and sometimes went to West Ham matches together.

When Ade rang Russell on his mobile to ask his advice, Russell knew it must be something serious. As Ade related the story of his visit to west London nightclub Movida, Russell became incensed. According to Ade, when he was refused entry, one of the bouncers taunted him with the words: 'What are you gonna do, you fucking cripple? You don't have any fucking legs.' Although Ade toyed with putting the incident down to experience, Russell was insistent it should get a wider airing and invited him on to his radio show to talk about what had happened.

During the interview, Russell made great play of naming the club as many times as he could to ensure maximum negative publicity, and described the bouncer as 'a grunting Neanderthal dragging this country back into the Stone Age with prejudice, ignorance and hatred'. Movida, however, strongly disputed the version of events, saying there were two sides to the story and that Ade had been abusive and aggressive.

When 6 Music bosses told Russell that the exchange had broken legal guidelines and could not be included in the programme's weekly podcast, Russell was furious. He informed them that if that was the case, then he didn't want the podcast released at all. Writing in *The Guardian*, Russell penned a blistering piece criticizing the BBC's decision, accusing them of taking the 'easiest option'. 'We didn't name anyone as being responsible and we could have given the club a right of reply,' he stormed. 'What Ade said made me really unhappy because he is my friend and a lovely person and I felt I was in a position to do something about what happened to him. I love that podcast and I really want it to work. But in my position, you spend so much time talking rubbish. It is not often you get to highlight an issue like this.' He signed off the article by saying: 'I understand the BBC's position; it must observe its internal code – but so must I, and so ought we all.' Somehow, the full unedited podcast still made its way to Russell's fan website, the Russell Brand Forum.

By midsummer, Russell seemed to be everywhere. As well as his radio, TV and journalistic commitments, he was continuing a gruelling stand-up tour, and preparing for the release of his first comedy DVD. The live show was especially important to Russell, who wanted to stress that he was more than a womanizing philanderer. As he told his radio listeners: 'I am good at comedy and I am getting a reputation as a hairy pervert.'

His schedule was hectic and he was exhausted. Although he had an overview of what was going on, day to day it seemed as if he was just following a timetable set down by his agent and PR team. The pressure meant that at times Russell could be snappy and impatient. In late July, he had stormed off stage at a gig at the Red Rose Club in Islington because some girls at the front of the venue were talking during his act, and he refused to come back on until they had left. When Russell returned, he blamed his meltdown on the fact he was feeling depressed. On another occasion, Russell admitted he went into 'a proper sulk' when the producer of the radio sitcom he was working on praised Trevor, but not him. According to Matt Morgan, there was also a tantrum when a new make-up artist applied his eyeliner to the inside of his eye rather than the outside.

During the rare moments he did have time off, he liked to chill out at home, catching up on DVDs and ordering vegetarian takeaways. If he could, he tried to make it to Focus 12 to help out. Wherever he went, he aimed to keep his body in balance with yoga.

Yet despite it all, Russell still wanted to push himself harder. Throughout the summer, he had been schmoozed by various top executives from the BBC and ITV. He was frustrated by the fact that he was still confined to digital channels with small audiences, such as E4 and 6 Music. But he knew he was treading a fine line between mass appeal and losing the risqué honesty he was famous for. In interviews, Russell was also keen to stress that he had more than paid his dues, and that he had now racked up considerable experience as a broadcaster. As he told *The Guardian*: 'I don't relish the idea of compromise particularly. I don't enjoy the fact that everything I do is preceded by the word digital. I am keen for as many people as possible to see my comedy.'

The Edinburgh Fringe had always been a highlight of the year for him. He found the audiences more receptive and women more 'sexy'. This time, Trevor was his opening act and they were looking forward to doing some more work on a surreal sketch show on which they were collaborating, called *Cloud Cuckoo Land*. Radio 2 and 6 Music controller Lesley Douglas was keen to experiment with the station's comedy programming, and there were plans to turn the venture into a series, and possibly even a TV show.

For the pilot, Russell and Trevor had really let their imaginations take flight. One skit was a visit to the doctor, retold as if it was a trip to an enchanted kingdom up Russell's rectum. In another, Trevor woke up in the morning after a date with a girl to find they had swapped legs. There was also a magic toilet that could flush people backwards in time.

The first episode was recorded in June. More material was added from some impromptu improvisation sessions at Russell's flat during the Edinburgh Fringe, and then performed in a hastily convened production. As Russell said: 'It's nice to do things on the hoof. You can over-prepare these things. We work together on most of the things we do.'

It was Matt's first visit to the Festival, so Russell found a two-bedroom flat for them to share for the ten-day run, five minutes away from the Assembly Rooms venue. Costing

£2,000 to rent, the newly decorated apartment was tastefully furnished with chandeliers and contemporary art.

Thanks to Russell's soaring profile, *Shame* was the hottest gig in Edinburgh. It received good reviews and tickets were selling for four times their face value. Despite his objection that his love life was all the tabloids were interested in, the stand-up show did nothing to dispel the image of Russell as a sex-mad womanizer. His subjects included how much he enjoyed deep-throat blow jobs and how he relished having objects inserted up his bottom.

Indeed, regardless of his new-found notoriety, there was no sign that Russell was toning down his sexual adventures. If anything, he was happy to admit he was taking advantage of the situation. As a celebrity, he acknowledged that the time it took to seduce a woman seemed to be inversely proportionate to how famous he got. Speaking to *GQ*, he revealed that whereas before, if he chatted up ten women, he could probably end up sleeping with two or three, now he could count on pulling eight or nine out of ten. Asked if he used prostitutes now, he said he had so many 'freebies' he didn't need to. He joked in his stand-up routine that his worst chat-up line was 'You – in the van'; though he stressed that whoever his conquests were, he always made sure that he treated the women he slept with 'nicely'. When he signed off his live shows, he had a message for the female members of the audience: 'Don't think I'm not accessible, just because I am on this stage. I am very accessible.' It was as good as an invitation for groupies to meet him afterwards in the bar.

However, there was a growing feeling in Russell's circle that it was time to rein in his promiscuity. Now he was a household name, they felt that he was opening himself up to accusations of predatory behaviour, or worse. There was no shortage of women lining up to sell their stories. So far, it had all been *Carry On*-style stuff – usually a description of Russell doing a silly dance in his underpants, a discussion of the size of Russell's penis and a review of his performance. But as long as he carried on sleeping around, he was at risk.

'I think a small part of Russell still hurts,' says one old friend, who has observed his womanizing at close hand. 'I don't think he enjoys the sex. I think he is trying to fill a void. When you have sex of that magnitude with that many people, there is a point of diminishing returns. If you love Belgian chocolate, you don't eat it until you can't taste any more.

'The phrase "quality control" also sprang to mind when you saw Russell with some of these women. I saw Russell with one of the girls who sold her story to the papers and she was a very average-looking lass. Russell just wanted to replace drugs with something that gave him the same endorphins. I don't think he was really enjoying it. I think he was filling in a gap. He was replacing one demon with another.'

Nevertheless, Russell was determined to enjoy himself at the Festival. Night after night, he would extend that open invitation to the single women in his audience to join him in the bar after the gig. Student Nadine Walker was among several who also accepted an offer to join Russell and his pals for a house party. She went back to his flat, and told *The Sun* she found three girls there already. She said Russell had led each of them away into the bedroom, always with the words: 'We have matters to discuss.' New Zealander Jen Smith was also invited back to the flat after she met Russell at the VIP bar in the city's Gilded Balloon venue. During their time together, Jen claimed that Russell had told her he had slept with a different woman every night.

Certainly, there was plenty of evidence that the £500,000 flat had seen some action when Russell and his friends departed at the end of the month. According to the horrified landlord, there were half-finished drinks, discarded scripts, cigarette butts and empty condom packets strewn about the property. There was even a used condom in one of the beds and a note addressed to Russell from a grateful groupie, which read: 'Thank you for having me – in more ways than one.'

Apart from a row over who was going to tidy up the mess, Russell thought no more of it as he headed back to London. On his return, he spent an evening with rock singer Courtney Love at her hotel. Russell had admired her performance in *Man on the Moon*, a biopic about the life of one of his comedy heroes, Andy Kaufman. Although Courtney was clearly enamoured with Russell, and gave him a necktie, Russell said they had kept it platonic.

Shortly afterwards, the comic flew off for a short holiday in Marrakech, so he could recharge his batteries before the launch of his new TV show for E4, *Russell Brand's Got Issues*. He had been on the go since the beginning of the year, and he now wanted some peace and quiet. When it became clear he wasn't going to get it at the large family hotel he checked into, he immediately left to find another place where he could lie by a swimming pool in peace.

His relaxation, however, was to be short-lived. Russell had been in Morocco only a few days when he was rung with the news that the police wanted to interview him about an alleged rape at his rented flat in Edinburgh. Russell was stunned. It was true that Trevor had pulled that night with a girl. The twenty-year-old brunette had met his sidekick when she had gone for a drink at the Tonic Bar after a gig. She had then gone to their flat on her own and, after spending the night with Trevor, she had seemed happy to stay for breakfast the next morning. As far as Russell was aware, nothing untoward had happened. Now she was alleging that she couldn't remember anything after she'd had a drink at the flat and was suggesting it might have been spiked. When she realized she had had sex, she had been advised by her friends to go to the police.

Russell knew it was nothing to do with him. Yet inevitably the news that police wanted to interview him to piece together what had happened that night was resulting in some alarming headlines, like 'Brand party "rape"' and '*Big Brother*'s Brand facing date-rape DNA probe'. In his absence, his PR team issued a strongly worded statement to clarify his involvement. 'It becomes necessary for Russell Brand to state he has no knowledge of, let alone any involvement in, the alleged assault of an Edinburgh woman,' the statement read. 'He understands a woman who, with a number of other people, visited his rented flat during the Edinburgh Fringe has made a complaint to the police. Mr Brand has no knowledge of what the complaint is about other than what has been published in the press.' It added that Russell was happy to talk to police when he returned from holiday.

So when Russell flew back for the *GQ* Awards ceremony in September, he was in a state of shock. Although he knew it was unlikely the claims would come to anything, he was concerned for Trevor, who was distraught. But he was also thrilled to have been nominated for a *GQ* award, and was hoping to bask in the glory of being named Britain's Most Stylish Man at the event that night.

No doubt his fellow award-winner Rod Stewart thought he was giving Russell some friendly advice when he approached him beforehand in the bar area to give him a pep talk about his womanizing ways. Russell listened politely, but privately felt it was a bit rich coming from a man who was almost as well known for his penchant for glamorous leggy blondes as he was for his music.

As Russell stepped on to the stage at the Royal Opera House to receive his gong from Lily Allen, he felt he had to address the rape allegation in some way. He tried to make light of it, venturing, 'I never did a sex attack. At the time, I was having consensual sex with witnesses – consensual, mind

– and a lovely evening it turned out to be.' Then, wisely changing the subject, he added: 'Here's to Rod Stewart, who had a go at me earlier this evening for too much womanizing. But then again, I did have a go on his daughter.'

The remark was a reference to a night Russell had spent with Rod's twenty-seven-year-old daughter Kimberly three months earlier. The pair had met when she had been a guest on *One Leicester Square* – and they had got on well during the interview. That evening, they went to the Cuckoo Club together, and Kimberly had been snapped looking cosy with Russell in the back of a cab. She admitted she had gone back to Russell's flat, but only because she had lost her keys, and she asserted that nothing sexual had taken place.

However, Russell's phrasing 'have a go' was ambiguous, and Rod was furious. Five minutes later, it was Rod's turn to take to the podium to collect an outstanding achievement award. When Rod approached the microphone, he fixed Russell with a glare. 'You went with my daughter, did you?' he barked. 'Were you well behaved, Russell? Stand up!'

With every eye in the auditorium on him, Russell felt he had no choice but to obey. Looking unusually ruffled, Russell mumbled: 'I took her out for one evening.' Stewart again demanded to know if Russell had behaved himself and Russell reassured him: 'I never touched that girl.' Happy he had forced a public confession, Rod added: 'So don't fucking say you did. It's not right. I am speaking as her father.'

Afterwards, Russell tried to brush it off, saying the matter was blown out of proportion and telling *Loaded* it was a 'light-hearted jape'. Guests who witnessed the altercation said there was nothing humorous about it. 'He might have claimed it was a laugh,' said one, 'but I was embarrassed for Russell and so was everyone else.'

Russell and Rod shared the same publicist and, for the sake of the cameras, they had a few words and posed for pictures. Gutted that his moment of glory had been tarnished, Russell left shortly afterwards. Yet Rod was unrepentant, ramming home his point by saying: 'Russell has been a bit timid since I said my bit. But he's got to be careful, he can't do what he did. He might be a bit of a player, but he mustn't boast like that. I never did.'

Two days later, Rod was still storming about the incident, telling journalists: 'Somebody had to put him in his place. We haven't made up – you can't go around saying things like that.' Meanwhile, Kimberly thanked her father for his gallant behaviour. 'I think he spoke rightly and he spoke completely truthfully, and he spoke as a father. It was really sweet. It took me by surprise, but I appreciated it. I had no idea he was going to say it. It was all real up there.'

But Russell had other things to worry about. The morning after the awards ceremony, he was not only waking up to reports of the spat in the papers. He was also facing an interview with Scottish police over what had happened in the Edinburgh flat. Somehow, he still managed to raise a smile for photographers when he turned up at John Noel's office to be interviewed with Trevor. During the two-hour grilling, Trevor conceded he'd had sex with the girl, but said as far as he was aware, the girl had been perfectly happy about it.

To make matters worse, in a Sunday newspaper kiss-and-tell, Coralie Robinson chose that moment to announce she was sleeping with Russell, but not exclusively. Russell admitted it. He did not elaborate on a report in the same article that said he had been in Morocco with a blonde fashion buyer by the name of Jessica Renton. Unusually for one of Russell's alleged conquests, Jessica declined to comment.

After such a difficult week, it was perhaps understandable that Russell sounded maudlin and depressed in an interview with *The Independent on Sunday* to promote *Russell Brand's Got Issues* on E4. It was a scattergun defence, in which he tackled the Dannii Minogue claim that he was a vile predator, and maintained that the exchange with Rod Stewart had been nothing but jokey banter blown totally out of proportion by the media. 'Even with things going this well, I ain't that happy. I am a bit sad,' he said, adding that he felt worn down by criticism. 'I really do care what people think about me. It really, really hurts my feelings when I read some things. I think: "Why would someone say that? And why would people believe that?" It makes me very sad that they're so judgemental.'

The ongoing rape allegation meant it was decided that it would be best if Trevor did not appear on the 10 and 17 September editions of the radio show. But Russell made his feelings plain by choosing innocence as the theme and telling listeners: 'The reason he's not here is obvious. Trevor emphatically denies the charges and if, and it's a big if, it goes to court, he will of course plead not guilty. He'll be back here before you know it, with his head held high.'

Since Russell's huge success in *Big Brother's Big Mouth*, Channel 4 had been looking for a vehicle for their new star. He had already shown himself to be a lively celebrity interviewer on MTV's *One Leicester Square. Big Mouth* had demonstrated that one of Russell's main strengths was interacting with ordinary members of the public and making them sound interesting. It was hoped that the format of *Russell Brand's Got Issues* would be the best of both worlds.

Originally, it had been entitled *The Now O'Clock Show*, but as Russell's stock started to rise, it seemed inconceivable that his name should be left out of the title. Russell would choose a theme every week, bring on a celebrity to talk about it, and then go to the audience for some reaction. The show was filmed in the afternoon at a rented studio at BBC headquarters in Wood Lane, in front of an audience of 150, and broadcast at 10.30 p.m. the same night.

Dubbed 'Topical Debate in Tight Trousers', the series was launched with vast publicity. There didn't seem to be a bus shelter in the land that didn't have pictures of a giant Russell looking down his nose and pounding his fist on the table of a Mad Hatter's tea party. The show was to run for at least six weeks on E4, before transferring to Channel 4.

The first programme, screened a week later than originally scheduled, on 12 September, was a typically anarchic Brand spectacle. It began with a stomach-churning sketch in which Russell played a pornography-reading grandfather figure, who eats the fake breasts of his baby grandson, played by Matt Morgan. To accompany the frenetic animated opening sequence which followed, Russell had chosen 'Deadwood', a track by his mate Carl Barat's band Dirty Pretty Things. The theme was: 'Is Our Lust for Beauty Making Us Ugly Human Beings?'

The show started with Russell silhouetted against a light box, brandishing a megaphone in a similar pose to one he had used in *Comedy Lab* back in 2003. He then launched into a monologue, in which he called for revolution and the creation of a new utopia.

The celebrity guest was Lily Allen, who had garnered almost as many column inches as Russell over the summer for her bad behaviour. But instead of being her usual gobby self, she looked like a bemused observer as Russell threw her coat into the crowd and a blind audience member stormed the couch to express her views on the subject. The show closed with a group of streakers running through the studio.

It had been chaotic, but oddly compelling television. Yet when the viewing figures came back, Russell was disappointed. Only 164,000 viewers tuned in for the debut programme, less than 1.4 per cent of the total TV audience. The episode of *Scrubs* in the same slot the week before had got 243,000 viewers. What hurt most was that little more than half the original audience – 83,000 viewers – returned the following week for the second show, with guest Laurence Llewelyn-Bowen.

The main criticism of the programme was that it was too superficial, a messy mishmash. Russell may have had issues, but with the ad breaks he had only twenty-three minutes to get to the bottom of them. The poor performance left Channel 4 executives utterly bemused, and Russell rattled. The 'It boy' presenter had been considered a sure bet for ratings success after the latest series of *Big Brother's Big Mouth* on E4 regularly pulled in over one million viewers. Reviews were also mixed. According to Jim Shelley of the *Mirror*: 'For uproarious enjoyment, not much beats *Russell Brand's Got Issues.*' Ian Hyland, the TV critic for the *News of the World*, summed up his verdict with devastating brevity. '*Russell Brand's Got Issues.* No. Russell Brand's got six months. Tops.'

It was clear that Russell needed to take drastic action to step up interest in the show and promote the fact that Jonathan Ross was due to feature as a guest. An interview with the *News of the World* was arranged, on condition that the programme was well publicized in the first few paragraphs. Acknowledging there were still things that could be refined, Russell said: 'It's good at the moment, but we're still perfecting it. When it's on Channel 4, it'll be really good.'

Russell had been interviewed by Jonathan Ross twice by this time – first on the established presenter's Radio 2 show, and then there was Russell's ground-breaking appearance on *Friday Night with Jonathan Ross* back in May. Now, Ross more than repaid the favour by appearing dressed up as Russell, admitting he had once had sex with a melon and that his fantasy was for his wife Jane to have sex on top of him, while eating jam doughnuts.

The comedy element of the series was also improving. The programme featured a funny sketch charting the course of Russell's relationship with his vacuum cleaner, Henry. The piece was actually filmed in Russell's flat, giving a glimpse of the most talked-about boudoir in London: Russell's very own bedroom.

Jonathan's appearance boosted the audience figures by 35,000 to 118,000 viewers. But by the time Russell had got to the fifth episode, there were rumblings that all was not well on the show. Reports of defections among the staff had reached the press. Director Dave Skinner, who had worked with Russell since his *Efourum* days, and a producer both left, with a TV insider telling the *Sunday Mirror*: 'The show hasn't taken off as expected. The departures have come as a shock. It's not a happy ship.' A spokeswoman said: 'Changes were made for editorial reasons.' Skinner refused to comment.

Chris Cowie, the former executive producer of *Top of the Pops*, was drafted in to help. By the final episode, it was generally agreed that the run had been a useful learning curve, but that a dramatic revamp was needed before it moved to Channel 4.

CHAPTER FOURTEEN

TALENT WILL OUT

'Russell Brand hosts the Oscars 2009 and presents himself with Best Actor.'

— RUSSELL IN *COMPANY* MAGAZINE, ON
HIS AMBITION FOR THE FUTURE, 2006

In less than a year, Russell's life had changed beyond all recognition. When he practised yoga, he had private lessons with Madonna's former teacher. The personal assistant he had hired to organize his life had once worked for American movie star Alec Baldwin. His house-sitter was shared with Steve Coogan. Every moment of his schedule was accounted for by his management and publicity teams. Even his vegetarian meals were delivered in a personalized box by bike to wherever he was in London.

As the hottest man in television, the money was also rolling in. Yet wealth had never been Russell's motivation. He was so disinterested that, every month, he simply got an allowance from his agent, so he didn't have to think about it. If Russell did spend cash on himself, it was often on clothes. These days, even his cardies were designer pieces costing £1,100 each.

His other indulgence was treatments. Although he was lusted over by millions of women, Russell was still not happy with the way he looked. Not only that, but to take his career to the next level, Russell felt he needed to iron out any niggling imperfections.

To sharpen up his appearance, he started a laser hair-removal course at a Harley Street clinic to get rid of any straggly hairs from his beard line. Russell even went to see a plastic surgeon about having some liposuction to suck out some of the fat from his hips so he'd look better in his skinny jeans. However, the doctor told him that there was nothing to remove, so instead Russell decided to tone up by going to a gym, in case he had to take his top off in any future film roles. Even though he had the most swooned-over pout in the country, Russell felt that that too could be improved. For a long time he had been self-conscious about his teeth, so he began wearing a retainer at all times, except when he was eating, doing yoga or broadcasting. If he lost it, he joked, it would probably end up on eBay.

One of the few things that remained the same had been his plain one-bedroom flat in Gospel Oak. But by the end of the year, Russell had started looking for a house in Primrose Hill, where prices started at around £2 million.

His wealth meant that he could afford to be generous to friends and family, paying for private medical treatment if they needed it, and generally making life more comfortable by offering to pay for anything that would otherwise stretch them.

Inevitably, Russell's success had also rubbed off on the most important person in his life, his mother. Babs still lived in the modest house in which she had brought up Russell. For the moment, moving out of the area was not on the cards because she wanted to stay close to her friends in Grays. Even so, Russell made sure she had all the luxuries he could shower her with. In the autumn, he bought her a sporty new Mini Cooper. Now she had reached sixty, he also assured her that he was financially secure enough for her not to have to work, so she gave up her job as a secretary in Stanford-le-Hope.

More than that, he wanted her to share in his limelight. Throughout the year, Russell made sure she was there for all of his most important moments, whether it was the filming of his comedy DVD or the start of a new programme. Each time, Babs turned up immaculately dressed, hair blow-dried, and beaming with pride. When she told him she liked *Strictly Come Dancing*, Russell arranged for her to be in the audience of the live show. However hectic the occasion, Russell's first concern was always that she was being well cared for. He would introduce her to his famous friends and, at the end of the evening, he would see her to her car and kiss her goodnight.

For Russell himself, one of the biggest benefits of stardom was that it gave him access to interesting people he wouldn't otherwise meet. Icons intrigued him. When he was introduced to a true celebrity in the flesh, in the shape of Tom Cruise, Keith Richards and even Terry Wogan, he would study them like a lepidopterist examining a new species of butterfly, dissecting their speech and body language as if to find the source of their charisma. It was as though Russell felt that to be elevated to the next stage of celebrity, there was a secret that he had to unlock.

Secret or no secret, there were already signs that Russell was moving into the ranks of the establishment. *The Times* called him a 'candidate national treasure'. He was thrilled in October when seasoned broadcaster Chris Evans anointed him as 'the voice of a generation'. As a tabloid fixture, his face was now a permanent feature in the backdrop of newsworthy people in *Have I Got News for You*. So recognizable was his look that people were going to Halloween parties dressed as him, and Avid Merrion and Rory Bremner paid him the ultimate compliment by parodying him.

Furthermore, Russell's arrival in the higher echelons of the comedy world was cemented when he was invited by Eddie Izzard to join the line-up for the revived Secret Policeman's Ball, in aid of Amnesty International, on 14 October. The 1979 show and its spin-off, the Secret Policeman's Other Ball, held two years later, had been iconic events, starring the cream of British comedy, from the Pythons to the *Not the Nine O'Clock News* team to French and Saunders. One of the highlights had been the legendary parody of the judge's summing-up in the Jeremy Thorpe trial by Russell's all-time hero, humorist Peter Cook.

It was a measure of how far Russell had come that he was one of the main attractions on the bill, which also included Graham Norton, *The Mighty Boosh*'s Noel Fielding and Julian Barratt, and Chevy Chase. Given the pressure of appearing alongside comedy greats, it was perhaps understandable that Russell stuck to some of his tried-and-tested material for part of his act, including a clinical dissection of an Ian Huntley story from *The Sun*, which was by now two years old.

Nonetheless, his routine went down a storm. Backstage after the gig, he bumped into Nigel Klarfeld, the manager who had helped discover him after the Hackney Empire New Act of the Year contest in 2000. Nigel, who had not seen Russell for six years, congratulated him warmly on his performance. 'I told him I thought he had done really well. Russell seemed genuinely pleased that I said it, as if he appreciated my approval. He was lovely, very friendly and polite.'

Among the others to commend him was Russell's close friend Vanessa Feltz, who messaged him after the show with her regards. Russell, who was thrilled by his reception on the night, cheekily replied: 'Could you celebrate my triumph by texting me a picture of your boobs?'

Russell's career achievements, remarkable though they were, were not his sole accomplishments that autumn. The working-class boy from Grays had also come up in the world. Not only was he picked as one of the 100 most eligible people by *Tatler* magazine, but Russell was also chosen to be in the new edition of *Debrett's People of the Year*, published by the arbiter of etiquette and manners since 1769. He was in good company, with Ricky Gervais, Victoria Beckham and former fling Kate Moss in the same exclusive coterie. The only difference was that Russell had been an A-list celebrity for a matter of months, while the rest had been famous for years. 'Society picks its icons in a way that no individual PR or media machine can fully control,' said a Debrett's spokesman. 'The people in the book have all shaped something this year, or done something particularly interesting. This is a celebration of our meritocratic society.'

Yet fame had not completely chased away the depression that had always dogged Russell. It was just that now the causes were different. He enjoyed the fact that the machinery of assistants, agents and broadcasting colleagues meant he never felt alone. But now he was a public figure, he was a target, and he often felt unfairly judged by people who had formed an opinion about him based on what he looked like, not on what he did.

Nor was fame a cure for the insecurities that hounded him. As he told radio listeners in October, he still felt 'rage' which dated back to his childhood – and even success couldn't erase it. 'That keeps bubbling up. I think it's a sense of sadness. I think that the pressures of becoming more famous are making me deeply unhappy.' With his workload so overwhelming, for the first time Russell also found himself suffering from psoriasis, which he blamed on stress.

There were now so many demands on him that Russell was candid enough to confess that he missed being able to use drugs to switch off his brain. It meant that he still felt it was very necessary for him to attend Alcoholics and Narcotics Anonymous groups for support. Russell admitted that he had originally planned to come off drugs only until his career was back on track. But these days, he knew there was no going back. He had too much to prove. Besides, even a frappuccino was enough to keep him awake all night.

In earlier days, when Russell had declared his ambition to be famous, people would warn him he would regret it one day when he couldn't walk down the street any more or go to the supermarket. Russell would reply that he didn't want to do either of those things anyway. He was fascinated by the effect his fame had and the way people held doors open for him now, as if he were an aristocratic lady. He remained as generous as ever when he was asked to pose for pictures or sign autographs, saying he enjoyed the ego boost. But the reality of his celebrity meant that he had to start wearing a woolly hat to West Ham matches and using the VIP loos. Otherwise, he got approached by so many fans, he missed the game.

The year had brought about one other important difference in Russell. At the start, he had no intention of getting involved in a long-term relationship. He told interviewers he was 'incapable' in any case, explaining that, 'I need to be constantly stimulated by new stuff.' In one article in the *Daily Star*, Russell was quoted as saying: 'I like what Lemmy from Motörhead said: "I've never met one that made me want to give up all the others."' Love to Russell was like a distant ideal, and not one he seemed in any hurry to achieve. 'It would be like salvation and redemption,' he told the *Sunday Herald*. 'I think it is innate within men to be pagan and to worship women, and I think one day I'll find a woman who will be the goddess, a return to the womb and eternal mother.'

After he had become famous, he had attempted to get back together with Amanda, who had been the only woman he ever really loved. They had tried to see if it would work, but then he told friends he had 'fucked it all up again'.

In November, as expected, the rape charge against Trevor was dropped. Nevertheless, the accusation against such a close friend had shaken Russell. He had already seen how much his own sex life was detracting from his comedy, which was still his priority. Now, Russell was determined to draw a clear line under his old ways, if he could. At first, he had found reading kiss-and-tells about himself 'hilarious'; it had become 'unbearable', and he caught himself imagining how any sexual encounter would sound if it ended up in a newspaper. Before, he would scan the audience for pretty girls he might want to chat up afterwards. Part of Russell felt liberated from the fact that after gigs he was no longer 'prowling around like a leopard man'.

Russell announced his change of heart abruptly on his 1 October radio show: 'The old womanizing is a fantasy and it exists no more. I have stopped having sex. Mostly because I am sick of reading about it and being constantly associated with it. It wasn't making me happy. It will last until I get married and have some children.'

A few days later, Russell went one step further by declaring he had a girlfriend, although in the interview with *The Guardian* website, it sounded rather like a career move. 'My intention is to shape my narrative. That is why I have to knock all that nonsense on the head. I have given women up. I have a girlfriend.'

Although the tabloids left it alone, the internet was awash with rumours about the girl's identity. Finally, she was revealed as nineteen-year-old Laura Gallacher. Russell had met her through her sister, TV presenter Kirsty, who was a stablemate at John Noel Management. Russell raved a few weeks later in *The Times*: 'I've got one girl now and it's lovely. She's an art student from a good family.' In fact, Laura was the privately educated daughter of former Ryder Cup champion Bernard Gallacher. It was hard to imagine someone more different from the Page Three girls he had previously dated.

There was one sticking point, though. Russell's aura of accessibility was an important part of his appeal to female fans. When, a couple of weeks later, Matt alluded to the mystery girlfriend on air, Russell joked: 'Shh, I don't have a girlfriend. Don't attack my core market.'

Even though his TV programme *Russell Brand's Got Issues* had not been a ratings hit, Russell's 6 Music show was a different matter. His headline-grabbing remarks had helped boost the audience of 6 Music by 40 per cent, from 285,000 listeners to a record 400,000. The phenomenon was even given a name: The Russell Brand Effect.

So it was a shock to read on the front page of the *Daily Star* on 2 November that Russell had been axed for being 'too insane' for the Sunday lunchtime slot. In fact, the story was only half right. Russell was leaving 6 Music – but to go over to the even more respectable climes of Radio 2.

For Russell, it was the realization of his hopes. Now that *Russell Brand's Got Issues* had finished its run on E4, he was looking forward to crossing over to Channel 4 at the end of November with a revamped and improved version. With the move to Radio 2 confirmed as well, it seemed his fervent wish to banish the word 'digital' from his career description had come true.

Russell's appointment to the radio station was the latest in a series of celebrity hirings it had made, all of which signified that it was determined to rid itself of its easy-listening, pipe-and-slippers image for good. 'It is the Hogwarts of radio. I just hope I can keep my wand up,' Russell said. 'Possibly I will be tongue-tied when I meet [Terry Wogan]. Radio 2 has a broad appeal, and [my transfer] is indicative of the direction that the station is taking. All I can do is do what I think is funny.'

Immediately, Radio 2's blogs were buzzing with the news. 'Russell Brand now? Dear God, whatever next?' raged one incensed listener. 'The list of programmes not to listen to grows ever longer. It's just another example of bringing in a celebrity for the sake of it, instead of worrying about what makes good radio.'

Middle England was certainly rattled. The announcement prompted a full-page debate in *The Daily Telegraph*. The *Daily Mail* launched into a rant, which was headlined: 'Drug Addict, Sex Addict, Bin Laden Impersonator. Is This Really What Radio 2 Needs?'

However, Gillian Reynolds, *The Telegraph*'s radio critic, pointed out that listeners had also 'moaned' about the arrival of Chris Evans before they had got used to him. 'This is a very shrewd move by Radio 2, which seems to be moving into what you would think of as Radio 1 territory,' she said. 'He has been very successful on radio and could transfer many twenty-something listeners with him.'

November was a key month for Russell for another reason, too. After months of planning, and some eleventh-hour hiccups, Russell was hosting a gig that was very close to his heart – a benefit night in aid of the rehab centre which had got him clean, Focus 12. His friend Noel Gallagher was to perform a rare acoustic set. At £50 a ticket, Russell had expected the audience to be made up of a rarefied group of music enthusiasts. What he found when he stepped out on to the stage of the Koko Club in Camden, north London, was a rabble of hard-core Oasis fans rowdier than a football crowd. When Noel's brother Liam appeared high up in a balcony box to view the show, like an emperor at the Colosseum, the mob went wild.

It had been a stressful twenty-four hours for Russell. There had been a last-minute panic when Kasabian's guitarist, Serge Pizzorno, was struck down with a bout of laryngitis and had to pull out. The day was saved by Russell's mate Carl Barat and the Dirty Pretty Things. Preferring to let the music do the talking, Russell was surprisingly subdued throughout the gig, watching intently from the sidelines.

As a reformed addict, it would have been easy to be pious. Yet Russell sensed it wasn't the time or place to talk about the evils of drugs, and hit the right note with risqué aplomb. 'I am not going to bore you with the fact that we are here to raise money, because the room smells of cannabis and cocaine,' he told the audience. 'This is about raising money to get people off drugs, when in the past all I used to raise was money to get drugs off people. Remember we are raising money for little junkies and all that. When you go outside in Camden, you will have to step over them.'

The raucous crowd meant that Russell had never been so

thankful to say the words: 'Welcome Noel Gallagher.' Backstage after the show, Russell was bowled over by his first meeting with Liam Gallagher, whom he also introduced to his mum Babs. Although he was mates with Noel, he had never met the Oasis frontman before. He was fascinated by Liam's raw charisma, which he described as a 'distillation of fame'.

By the end of the evening, Russell looked relieved, although the event was marred by the fact that a thief had got into his dressing room and stolen his £800 coat. Russell went into a sulk, and even when a friend reminded him that the whole gig could not have happened without him, a maudlin Russell merely replied: 'If I had kept a diary, then Thursday's entry would read, "Thursday: my coat was stolen!"' But come the next day, his spirits were lifted by the news that the benefit had raised £100,000 for the centre.

Saturday 17 November saw his debut show for Radio 2 – before which he gave some final reassurance to the more sedate listeners. 'Do not be alarmed, I will respect your radio station, promise,' Russell wrote on the website before the programme went on air. 'Nah, don't worry, it's all going to be a right proper lovely old laugh. Think of me as the new substitute teacher, but don't be tempted to be horrible and victimize me, give me a chance – and for Gawd's sake, look after me!'

Although an hour shorter, the format was unchanged from the 6 Music programme. It was still the same three-way banter between Russell, Trevor and Matt – but this time, with a bit more restraint and more received pronunciation. As ever, Noel Gallagher called in and hit the nail on the head: 'Listening to the radio on Saturday night, it's like being in the war. It's a lot less boisterous this week. You are turning into Whispering Russell Brand.'

Russell, however, maintained he was only biding his time; as the weeks went on, he relaxed into the role. His own celebrity status meant he was able to attract big-name guests, and in the first three weeks pulled off interviews with *Little Britain* stars David Walliams and Matt Lucas, and also with Courtney Love, who still appeared to be holding a candle for him after they had met several months earlier. His tour de force was an hour-long interview with his idol Morrissey, who seemed at turns to be both flattered by and disdainful of Russell's hero-worship.

Perhaps the funniest moment of the first few broadcasts was when Matt Lucas told Russell that Kate Moss would be in attendance at the forthcoming *Little Britain* Comic Relief event, at which Russell was also scheduled to appear, and asked, 'Have you met her in real life?' Russell took a diplomatic sidestep, saying: 'Blimey, the excitement of it all,' before adding, 'I met her very briefly. She's a lovely, lovely person.'

Nonetheless, it was hard for the imagination not to go into overdrive picturing the scene between Russell and Kate backstage. In fact, Russell revealed to Robert Crampton of *The Times* that he and Kate had got over their differences dating back to their brief liaison. 'She's a friend,' said Russell. 'I think she is lovely and Pete [Doherty] is lovely and I think it would be good if they were together and happy and looking after one another.'

Overall, reviews of the new Radio 2 show were glowing, with most of the national newspapers weighing in with their opinions. *The Guardian*'s Elisabeth Mahoney was hopeful the programme would shake up the station – although she noted the more sedate pace. 'The best material was the interaction between Brand and his on-air team, and Brand's verbal adventures in playful incongruity,' she wrote.

Miranda Sawyer of *The Observer*, meanwhile, also loved Russell's winning turn of phrase, adding that: 'Brand is also, à la Jonathan Ross, divertingly self-aware, taking the mickey out of himself as much as do his compadres. Did I mention that he's very funny? His two-hour show quite brightened up my Saturday night in.'

Having told Radio 2 listeners to reserve their judgement until they had heard Russell for themselves, *The Telegraph*'s reviewer Gillian Reynolds heaped on further praise, saying that while Russell was 'a pain' on television, he was 'an original' on radio. 'I originally thought this show was intended for girls getting ready to go out. I realize now it's more for people staying in, looking for a bit of a think and a cuddle. It's addictive,' she concluded.

As the winter set in, Russell wanted to tie up some loose ends and settle some old scores. The *Daily Star* apologized for a headline, which implied that Russell was to be questioned as a suspect in the alleged Edinburgh rape, even though he was only ever viewed as a potential witness. In a self-penned article in *Red* magazine, Russell also sought to set the record straight on his relationship with Sadie Frost, saying that although at times he had considered giving her 'a saucy cuddle', they were just friends.

In particular, Russell wanted to challenge the preconceptions that he felt had unfairly grown up around him. His tabloid image was nothing to do with him, he claimed. It was all beyond his control. The person in the papers was like 'his conjoined twin', he asserted, who had broken away from him and was 'arsing around and causing all this hullabaloo'. His favourite subject now became a discourse on how tabloids 'abstract you from yourself'.

Most importantly, he wanted to get across the fact that he was a different person from what people had been led to believe by the kiss-and-tell exposés. 'I read them things and think, "I'm nice. I am not a bad person. I'm a good person to my friends,"' he told *The Word*. 'Yes, I am vain. Yes, I have an ego. Yes, I'm ambitious. But I am also gentle and considerate and sensitive and caring. I am not some big, horrible, ugly, swaggering, braggart … pirate.

'It's all meaningless guff and I understand how it might make people think: "Flash in the pan, he'll be down with the Christmas decorations," but I have worked really hard.'

After so much coverage of other kinds, Russell felt it was imperative to remind people that what he was, first and foremost, was a comedian. For that reason, he wanted his DVD *Russell Brand Live* to capture the best possible performance and cement his arrival as Britain's most important stand-up. The film was shot at the Shepherd's Bush Empire on two nights in October, in front of a star-studded audience, and released in time for the festive shopping spree. Wielding a gold-plated microphone lead, which he whipped around the stage in tribute to Morrissey, Russell dissected the press image of himself, portraying himself as a philandering Frank Spencer. Comedy reviewers noted that although much of the material was now familiar to devoted fans, it was Russell's ad-libs off camera which generated the biggest laughs; observing that it was his skill as an improviser that pointed to the fact that Russell was a real talent who was going to be around for a very long time.

There was to be one more dip in the rollercoaster of Russell's career before the year was over. Russell was taken aback to be told that his MTV show, *One Leicester Square,* would be axed at the end of 2006. The decision had nothing to do with Russell, who had done a good job. It was a cost issue. The programme was very expensive to produce, but had not won good ratings, and the American bosses felt the cash would be better spent on formats they knew had worked in the US. 'There is no way that anyone in their right mind would get rid of Russell if they could afford him,' said an MTV insider. 'We didn't see much of him, but Russell was very well liked. There had been a genuine affection for him. The only problem with him was that he was getting massively overcommitted. It became simply impossible to tie his schedule down because you were fighting against five or six different people.'

Russell was disappointed, but felt that at least he could now devote more time to making his new Channel 4 show a success. As part of its transfer to the terrestrial channel, the programme was expanded to fifty minutes and conducted in a more intimate, nightclub-type atmosphere. The revamp was underlined by the fact that the 'Got Issues' element of the title was dropped altogether, in favour of the straightforward, make-no-mistake name *The Russell Brand Show*.

Friday night at 11.05 p.m. was always going to be a tough time slot. Ironically, for the first half-hour Russell would be waging a ratings battle against the man who had helped bring him to prominence in the first place, Jonathan Ross. Matt Morgan had been promoted to creative director on the show, and there was now scope for some of their more absurd comic ideas, including mocked-up CCTV footage claiming to show the bizarre behaviour of celebrity guests in their dressing rooms before they came on.

In the early episodes, the series retained its experimental feel, as if Russell was still trying to sort out what worked and what didn't. The initial viewing figures were around 500,000, about 4 per cent of the total TV audience. Jonathan Ross was the big boy, pulling in a steady 3.8 million and a quarter of the audience for the BBC. Still, Russell had increased Channel 4's Friday night share by 200,000, and he felt the programme would soon hit its stride, although he also admitted that it was tough to get good guests. But as Russell was quoted as saying in *The Observer*, Jonathan Ross's first show was not an immediate hit. '*The Last Resort* was not witnessed by a terribly high number of people. And look at him now.'

A continuing stream of industry accolades gave Russell some reassurance that his comedy was getting recognized, and that he was not just a figment of the tabloid imagination. He had kicked off 2006 by winning the *Time Out* award for Stand-Up Comedian of the Year; after that, he'd clocked up further gongs for *GQ*'s Most Stylish Man, and the Funniest Man from *Loaded* magazine.

But there were two more trophies he truly wanted for his mantelpiece – the British Comedy Awards for Best Live Stand-Up Tour and Best Male Newcomer. He garnered nominations for both in December. The official presentation ceremony was held at the South Bank studios in London and compered by Jonathan Ross. Regrettably, the evening was soured for Russell by the host's remark that, 'Everyone seems to know everything about him [Russell] – apart from when his show is on,' and the surprising decision to give Russell's comedy antithesis, the aloof Jimmy Carr, the coveted award for Best Live Stand-Up Tour, despite the critical acclaim that Russell had received for his gigs.

Instead, Russell went home with the gong for Best Male Newcomer for his work on *Russell Brand's Got Issues* – even though it was probably his least successful venture. As he took to the podium, he joked: 'It's nice to be acknowledged for comedy, but I must preserve my energy as I'm also up for *The Sun*'s Shagger of the Year award.'

Indeed, amid intense competition from Calum Best and James Blunt, he won the title a few days later. Despite his determination to break free from his playboy image, Russell was amused rather than offended – and accepted the prize with good grace.

As 2006 drew to a close, no year-end round-up was complete without a description of Russell's dramatic ascent up the celebrity ladder. If he hadn't been appearing as a contestant on Channel 4's *Big Fat Quiz of the Year* in late December, he would probably have been a category in his own right. For the two-hour show, he was paired with comedy goth twin Noel Fielding from *The Mighty Boosh*. The duo hit it off once again, having previously ad-libbed for the cameras backstage at the Secret Policeman's Ball in October. Now, up against the opposing team of Jonathan Ross and David Walliams, Russell and Noel were like a pair of irreverent schoolboys, throwing one-liners like paper darts from the back of the classroom. It said much about the way Russell polarized opinion that while he was stealing the limelight on the Channel 4 quiz, over on the BBC he was simultaneously being named as the third most irritating person of the year, after Pete Doherty and Nikki from *Big Brother 7*.

With just a short break before *Celebrity Big Brother* started in early January 2007, Russell headed off on holiday to Mauritius. For the past twelve months, he had barely stopped for breath, excepting his quick trip to Morocco. When he hadn't been presenting TV and radio shows, he had been hitting the headlines with his sex life, doing stand-up, arranging charity benefits or staying on the wagon at AA and NA meetings. Though at times he had been beside himself with fatigue, he'd felt he needed to keep going to justify his fame and to ensure that there was no going back.

When photographs of Russell's holiday appeared in the papers, they were scenes that could have come straight from a piss-take by Matt and Trevor. Russell was snapped in his skimpy black speedos, hair demurely tucked up in a bun, reclining on a sunlounger. All that was missing was a cocktail with an umbrella and a cherry. To complete the slightly comic picture, Russell had not only taken his girlfriend Laura with him – but also his mum Babs. Russell had stayed true to his word about his new lifestyle. His relationship with Laura was now in its third month: as the *Sunday Mirror* remarked, 'Aeons on Planet Brand.'

As he finally found the time to unwind, Russell had a lot to look back on. He had started the year as a little-known digital

TV presenter and ended up on the verge of the entertainment A-list. His dandy outfits and camped-up voice still attracted lust and derision in equal measure. The under-thirties loved him. For the most part, their parents hated him. But at least everyone had a view.

In many ways, he was a more thoughtful figure than he had been when he'd exploded on to the scene at the start of the year. Some of the bravado and the swagger seemed to have gone. To begin with, Russell had been like an adolescent, who hadn't known how little he really knew about life until he had lived it. If he had learned anything in the past year, it was perhaps to be careful what he wished for.

If it was possible, 2007 looked even more hectic for Russell. To start with, there was *Celebrity Big Brother*, and another stint on *Big Brother's Big Mouth*. Then, in just a few weeks' time, he had the job of singlehandedly reviving Britain's biggest music awards ceremony, the BRITs. The last time the event had been broadcast live, eighteen years ago, it had gone down in history as one of the most shambolic productions in the annals of TV, thanks to presenters Mick Fleetwood and Sam Fox. Now, Russell was to be the first host to present it live once again, on 14 February – and already he was predicting high drama. 'Once it starts, it is all in my hands,' he promised. 'It is going to be like the rock-and-roll BRITs of old, returned to the controlled mayhem and danger. I am going to be the ringleader at this carnival. I'm really looking forward to it.'

If 2006 had been the year when people had finally woken up to his comedy, then it was likely that 2007 would be the year when his ability as an actor would be recognized. In April, *Penelope*, the film in which he had appeared with Christina Ricci, was due for release, marking Russell's first foray into Hollywood. The movie had been acclaimed at the Toronto Film Festival and Russell was hopeful that it would bring about many more acting opportunities. Other, substantial roles were already being talked about – including a starring part in a biopic of pop star Adam Ant, based on the singer's autobiography *Stand and Deliver*. It was felt the pair shared the same rock-star looks and troubled childhoods.

But if ever there was a role tailor-made for Russell, it was his part in a new pilot for an ITV1 comedy, *The Abbey*. He was to play a drug addict in a sitcom set in a rehab centre, which was loosely based on real-life treatment site, the Priory. If the pilot show proved a hit, it would become a series. Russell had once again come full circle. The production company was Baby Cow, Steve Coogan's firm, which had made *Cruise of the Gods*, the Christmas comedy special from which he had been spectacularly fired back in 2002.

Just five years earlier, Russell had been a drug addict whose narcotic haze meant he hadn't even turned up to some of the programmes he was supposed to be presenting. Yet now, even though he had successfully fronted four different shows in the last year, Russell still felt he had a great deal to prove. To fit everything in, he was a focused workaholic who would rise at 5 a.m. to write his *Guardian* column, and who would spend any spare time between broadcasting commitments touring the country doing stand-up gigs.

Undoubtedly, this was Russell's moment, and he wasn't going to let it slip away. Despite hours of performances, whole rainforests' worth of column inches, and wide-ranging accomplishments across countless media, he said frankly to *The Word*: 'No one's seen what I can do yet.'

For Russell, this is just the first phase of his career. He is so driven that he is the first to admit that he will never be satisfied with what he has achieved. As far as Russell Brand is concerned, he hasn't even started.

SOURCES

As well as nearly 100 one-to-one interviews, the following have been helpful in tracing the course of Russell's life and career. Many thanks to the following newspapers, magazines, websites, radio stations, books and DVDs.

BOOKS

Pearce, Simon (ed.), *That Which Is Not Said: A Collection of Comics' Poetry* (Look at You, 2006)

DVDS

Russell Brand Live (Universal Pictures Video, 2006)

MAGAZINES

Broadcast
Channel 4 Magazine
Closer
Company
Cosmopolitan
Elle
Glamour
GQ
Heat
More
NME Student Guide
Now
Red
Time Out
TV and Satellite Week
The Word

NEWSPAPERS

Belfast Telegraph
Birmingham Post
Bury Free Press
Celebs on Sunday
Daily Mail

Daily Mirror
Daily Record
Daily Star
The Daily Telegraph
Evening Standard
Fest
Glasgow Herald
The Guardian
The Independent on Sunday
Liverpool Echo
Metro
The Morning Star
Newcastle Journal
News of the World
The Observer
The People
Press Association
Scotland on Sunday
The Scotsman
The Stage
The Sun
Sunday Herald
Sunday Mail
Sunday Mirror
Three Weeks
Thurrock Gazette
The Times

RADIO STATIONS

BBC 6 Music
BBC Radio 2
XFM

WEBSITES

www.bbc.co.uk
www.chortle.co.uk
www.focus12.co.uk
www.johnnoelmanagement.com
www.pilkipedia.co.uk
www.russellbrandfansite.com
www.russellbrand.tv
www.xfm.co.uk